The Pirates of Penzance by Gilbert & Sullivan

or, The Slave of Duty

Libretto by William S. Gilbert
Music by Arthur Sullivan

The partnership between William Schwenck Gilbert and Arthur Seymour Sullivan and their canon of Savoy Operas is rightly lauded by all lovers of comic opera the world over.

Gilbert's sharp, funny words and Sullivan's deliciously lively and hummable tunes create a world that is distinctly British in view but has the world as its audience.

Both men were exceptionally talented and gifted in their own right and wrote much, often with other partners, that still stands the test of time. However, together as a team they created Light or Comic Operas of a standard that have had no rivals equal to their standard, before or since. That's quite an achievement.

To be recognised by the critics is one thing but their commercial success was incredible. The profits were astronomical, allowing for the building of their own purpose built theatre – The Savoy Theatre.

Beginning with the first of their fourteen collaborations, Thespis in 1871 and travelling through many classics including The Sorcerer (1877), H.M.S. Pinafore (1878), The Pirates of Penzance (1879), The Mikado (1885), The Gondoliers (1889) to their finale in 1896 with The Grand Duke, Gilbert & Sullivan created a legacy that is constantly revived and admired in theatres and other media to this very day.

Index of Contents

To prevent unauthorized versions of this opera Gilbert & Sullivan decided to present official versions of this by opening simultaneously in England and America. It debuted on December 31, 1879 at the Fifth Avenue Theater in New York with Sullivan himself conducting. A single performance had been given on the previous day at the Royal Bijou Theatre, Paignton, England, to secure the British copyright.

On April 3, 1880, the Pirates of Penzance began its long run of 363 performances at the Opéra Comique in London.

DRAMATIS PERSONAE

MAJOR-GENERAL STANLEY
THE PIRATE KING
SAMUEL (his Lieutenant)
SERGEANT OF POLICE
MABEL, EDITH, KATE, and ISABEL (General Stanley's Daughters)
RUTH (a Pirate Maid of all Work)
Chorus of Pirates, Police, and General Stanley's Daughters

SCENES
ACT I - A rocky sea-shore on the coast of Cornwall
ACT II - A ruined chapel by moonlight

MUSICAL NUMBERS
Overture (includes "With cat-like tread", "Ah, leave me not to pine", "Pray observe the magnanimity",
"When you had left our pirate fold", "Climbing over rocky mountain", and "How beautifully blue the
sky")
ACT I
1. Pour, oh pour, the pirate sherry (Samuel and Chorus of Pirates)
2. When Fred'ric was a little lad (Ruth)
3. Oh, better far to live and die (Pirate King and Chorus of Pirates)
4. Oh! false one, you have deceiv'd me (Frederic and Ruth)
5. Climbing over rocky mountain (Chorus of Girls)
6. Stop, ladies, pray (Edith, Kate, Frederic, and Chorus of Girls)
7. Oh, is there not one maiden breast? (Frederic and Chorus of Girls)
8. Poor wand'ring one (Mabel and Chorus of Girls)
9. What ought we to do? (Edith, Kate, and Chorus of Girls)
10. How beautifully blue the sky (Mabel, Frederic, and Chorus of Girls)
11. Stay, we must not lose our senses ... Here's a first-rate opportunity to get married with impunity
(Frederic and Chorus of Girls and Pirates)
12. Hold, monsters (Mabel, Major-General, Samuel, and Chorus)
13. I am the very model of a modern Major-General (Major-General and Chorus)
14. Finale Act I (Mabel, Kate, Edith, Ruth, Frederic, Samuel, King, Major-General, and Chorus)
Oh, men of dark and dismal fate
I'm telling a terrible story
Hail, Poetry
Oh, happy day, with joyous glee
Pray observe the magnanimity (reprise of Here's a first-rate opportunity)
ACT II
15. Oh, dry the glist'ning tear (Mabel and Chorus of Girls)
16. Then, Frederic, let your escort lion-hearted (Frederic and Major-General)
17. When the foeman bares his steel (Mabel, Edith, Sergeant, and Chorus of Policemen and Girls)
18. Now for the pirates' lair! (Frederic, Ruth, and King)
19. When you had left our pirate fold [The paradox trio] (Ruth, Frederic, and King)
20. Away, away! My heart's on fire! (Ruth, Frederic, and King)
21. All is prepar'd; your gallant crew await you (Mabel and Frederic)

22. Stay, Fred'ric, stay ... Ah, leave me not to pine ... Oh, here is love, and here is truth (Mabel and Frederic)
23. No, I'll be brave ... Though in body and in mind (Reprise of When the foeman bares his steel) (Mabel, Sergeant, and Chorus of Police)
23a. Sergeant, approach! (Mabel, Sergeant of Police, and Chorus of Police)
24. When a felon's not engaged in his employment (Sergeant and Chorus of Police)
25. A rollicking band of pirates we (Sergeant and Chorus of Pirates and Police)
26. With cat-like tread, upon our prey we steal (Samuel and Chorus of Pirates and Police)
27. Hush, hush, not a word! (Frederic, King, Major-General, and Chorus of Police and Pirates)
28. Finale, Act II (Ensemble)
Sighing softly to the river
Now what is this, and what is that?
You/We triumph now
Away with them, and place them at the bar!
Poor wandering ones!

ACT I

(Scene.-A rocky seashore on the coast of Cornwall. In the distance is a calm sea, on which a schooner is lying at anchor. Rock L. sloping down to L.C. of stage. Under these rocks is a cavern, the entrance to which is seen at first entrance L. A natural arch of rock occupies the R.C. of the stage.

As the curtain rises groups of pirates are discovered — some drinking, some playing cards. SAMUEL, the Pirate Lieutenant, is going from one group to another, filling the cups from a flask. FREDERIC is seated in a despondent attitude at the back of the scene. RUTH kneels at his feet.)

OPENING CHORUS

ALL
Pour, O pour the pirate sherry;
Fill, O fill the pirate glass;
And, to make us more than merry
Let the pirate bumper pass.

SAMUEL
For today our pirate 'prentice
Rises from indentures freed;
Strong his arm, and keen his scent is
He's a pirate now indeed!

ALL
Here's good luck to Fred'ric's ventures!
Fred'ric's out of his indentures.

SAMUEL
Two and twenty, now he's rising,

And alone he's fit to fly,
Which we're bent on signalizing
With unusual revelry.

ALL
Here's good luck to Fred'ric's ventures!
Fred'ric's out of his indentures.
Pour, O pour the pirate sherry;
Fill, O fill the pirate glass;
And, to make us more than merry
Let the pirate bumper pass.

(FREDERIC rises and comes forward with PIRATE KING, who enters)

KING
Yes, Frederic, from to-day you rank as a full-blown
member of our band.

ALL
Hurrah!

FREDERIC
My friends, I thank you all, from my heart, for your
kindly wishes. Would that I could repay them as they
deserve!

KING
What do you mean?

FREDERIC
To-day I am out of my indentures, and to-day I leave
you for ever.

KING
But this is quite unaccountable; a keener hand at
scuttling a Cunarder or cutting out a White Star never
shipped a handspike.

FREDERIC
Yes, I have done my best for you. And why? It was my
duty under my indentures, and I am the slave of duty.
As a child I was regularly apprenticed to your band.
It was through an error — no matter, the mistake was
ours, not yours, and I was in honour bound by it.

SAMUEL
An error? What error? (RUTH rises and comes forward)

FREDERIC

I may not tell you; it would reflect upon my well-loved
Ruth.

RUTH

Nay, dear master, my mind has long been gnawed by the
cankering tooth of mystery. Better have it out at
once.

SONG — **RUTH**

RUTH

When Frederic was a little lad he proved so brave and daring,
His father thought he'd 'prentice him to some career seafaring.
I was, alas! his nurs'rymaid, and so it fell to my lot
To take and bind the promising boy apprentice to a pilot —
A life not bad for a hardy lad, though surely not a high lot,
Though I'm a nurse, you might do worse than make your boy a pilot.
I was a stupid nurs'rymaid, on breakers always steering,
And I did not catch the word aright, through being hard of hearing;
Mistaking my instructions, which within my brain did gyrate,
I took and bound this promising boy apprentice to a pirate.
A sad mistake it was to make and doom him to a vile lot.
I bound him to a pirate — you! — instead of to a pilot.
I soon found out, beyond all doubt, the scope of this disaster,
But I hadn't the face to return to my place, and break it to my master.
A nurs'rymaid is not afraid of what you people call work,
So I made up my mind to go as a kind of piratical maid-of-all-work.
And that is how you find me now, a member of your shy lot,
Which you wouldn't have found, had he been bound apprentice to a pilot.

RUTH:

Oh, pardon! Frederic, pardon! (Kneels)

FREDERIC

Rise, sweet one, I have long pardoned you. (RUTH rises)

RUTH

The two words were so much alike!

FREDERIC:

They were. They still are, though years have rolled over their heads. But this afternoon my obligation
ceases. Individually, I love you all with affection unspeakable; but, collectively, I look upon you with a
disgust that amounts to absolute detestation. Oh! Pity me, my beloved friends, for such is my sense of
duty that, once out of my indentures, I shall feel myself bound to devote myself heart and soul to your
extermination!

ALL

Poor lad — poor lad! (All weep)

KING
Well, Frederic, if you conscientiously feel that it is your duty to destroy us, we cannot blame you for acting on that conviction. Always act in accordance with the dictates of your conscience, my boy, and chance the consequences.

SAMUEL
Besides, we can offer you but little temptation to remain with us. We don't seem to make piracy pay. I'm sure I don't know why, but we don't.

FREDERIC
I know why, but, alas! I mustn't tell you; it wouldn't be right.

KING
Why not, my boy? It's only half-past eleven, and you are one of us until the clock strikes twelve.

SAMUEL
True, and until then you are bound to protect our interests.

ALL
Hear, hear!

FREDERIC
Well, then, it is my duty, as a pirate, to tell you that you are too tender-hearted. For instance, you make a point of never attacking a weaker party than yourselves, and when you attack a stronger party you invariably get thrashed.

KING
There is some truth in that.

FREDERIC
Then, again, you make a point of never molesting an orphan!

SAMUEL
Of course: we are orphans ourselves, and know what it is.

FREDERIC
Yes, but it has got about, and what is the consequence? Every one we capture says he's an orphan. The last three ships we took proved to be manned entirely by orphans, and so we had to let them go. One would think that Great Britain's mercantile navy was recruited solely from her orphan asylums — which we know is not the case.

SAMUEL
But, hang it all! you wouldn't have us absolutely merciless?

FREDERIC
There's my difficulty; until twelve o'clock I would, after twelve I wouldn't. Was ever a man placed in so

delicate a situation?

RUTH
And Ruth, your own Ruth, whom you love so well, and who has won her middle-aged way into your boyish heart, what is to become of her?

KING
Oh, he will take you with him.

FREDERIC
Well, Ruth, I feel some difficulty about you. It is true that I admire you very much, but I have been constantly at sea since I was eight years old, and yours is the only woman's face I have seen during that time. I think it is a sweet face.

RUTH
It is — oh, it is!

FREDERIC
I say I think it is; that is my impression. But as I have never had an opportunity of comparing you with other women, it is just possible I may be mistaken.

KING
True.

FREDERIC
What a terrible thing it would be if I were to marry this innocent person, and then find out that she is, on the whole, plain!

KING
Oh, Ruth is very well, very well indeed.

SAMUEL
Yes, there are the remains of a fine woman about Ruth.

FREDERIC
Do you really think so?

SAMUEL
I do

FREDERIC
Then I will not be so selfish as to take her from you. In justice to her, and in consideration for you, I will leave her behind.

(Hands RUTH to KING)

KING

No, Frederic, this must not be. We are rough men, who lead a rough life, but we are not so utterly heartless as to deprive thee of thy love. I think I am right in saying that there is not one here who would rob thee of this inestimable treasure for all the world holds dear.

ALL (loudly)
Not one!

KING
No, I thought there wasn't. Keep thy love, Frederic, keep thy love.

(Hands her back to FREDERIC)

FREDERIC
You're very good, I'm sure.

(Exit RUTH)

KING
Well, it's the top of the tide, and we must be off. Farewell, Frederic. When your process of extermination begins, let our deaths be as swift and painless as you can conveniently make them.

FREDERIC
I will! By the love I have for you, I swear it! Would that you could render this extermination unnecessary by accompanying me back to civilization!

KING
No, Frederic, it cannot be. I don't think much of our profession, but, contrasted with respectability, it is comparatively honest. No, Frederic, I shall live and die a Pirate King.

SONG — **PIRATE KING**

KING
Oh, better far to live and die
Under the brave black flag I fly,
Than play a sanctimonious part
With a pirate head and a pirate heart.
Away to the cheating world go you,
Where pirates all are well-to-do;
But I'll be true to the song I sing,
And live and die a Pirate King.
For I am a Pirate King!
And it is, it is a glorious thing
To be a Pirate King!
For I am a Pirate King!

ALL
You are!
Hurrah for the Pirate King!

KING
And it is, it is a glorious thing
To be a Pirate King.

ALL
It is!
Hurrah for the Pirate King!
Hurrah for the Pirate King!

KING
When I sally forth to seek my prey
I help myself in a royal way.
I sink a few more ships, it's true,
Than a well-bred monarch ought to do;
But many a king on a first-class throne,
If he wants to call his crown his own,
Must manage somehow to get through
More dirty work than e'er I do,
For I am a Pirate King!
And it is, it is a glorious thing
To be a Pirate King!
For I am a Pirate King!

ALL
You are!
Hurrah for the Pirate King!

KING
And it is, it is a glorious thing
To be a Pirate King.

ALL
It is!
Hurrah for the Pirate King!
Hurrah for the Pirate King!

(Exeunt all except FREDERIC. Enter RUTH.)

RUTH
Oh, take me with you! I cannot live if I am left behind.

FREDERIC
Ruth, I will be quite candid with you. You are very dear to me, as you know, but I must be circumspect. You see, you are considerably older than I. A lad of twenty-one usually looks for a wife of seventeen.

RUTH
A wife of seventeen! You will find me a wife of a thousand!

FREDERIC

No, but I shall find you a wife of forty-seven, and that is quite enough. Ruth, tell me candidly and without reserve: compared with other women, how are you?

RUTH

I will answer you truthfully, master: I have a slight cold, but otherwise I am quite well.

FREDERIC

I am sorry for your cold, but I was referring rather to your personal appearance. Compared with other women, are you beautiful?

RUTH (bashfully)
I have been told so, dear master.

FREDERIC
Ah, but lately?

RUTH
Oh, no; years and years ago.

FREDERIC
What do you think of yourself?

RUTH
It is a delicate question to answer, but I think I am a fine woman.

FREDERIC
That is your candid opinion?

RUTH
Yes, I should be deceiving you if I told you otherwise.
FREDERIC
Thank you, Ruth. I believe you, for I am sure you would not practice on my inexperience. I wish to do the right thing, and if- I say if- you are really a fine woman, your age shall be no obstacle to our union! (Shakes hands with her. Chorus of girls heard in the distance, "climbing over rocky mountain," etc.) Hark! Surely I hear voices! Who has ventured to approach our all but inaccessible lair? Can it be Custom House? No, it does not sound like Custom House.

RUTH (aside)
Confusion! it is the voices of young girls! If he should see them I am lost.

FREDERIC
(looking off) By all that's marvellous, a bevy of beautiful maidens!

RUTH (aside)
Lost! lost! lost!

FREDERIC

How lovely, how surpassingly lovely is the plainest of them! What grace- what delicacy- what refinement! And Ruth— Ruth told me she was beautiful!

RECITATIVE

FREDERIC
Oh, false one, you have deceived me!

RUTH
I have deceived you?

FREDERIC
Yes, deceived me!
(Denouncing her.)

FREDERIC
You told me you were fair as gold!

RUTH (wildly)
And, master, am I not so?

FREDERIC
And now I see you're plain and old.

RUTH
I'm sure I'm not a jot so.

FREDERIC
Upon my innocence you play.

RUTH
I'm not the one to plot so.

FREDERIC
Your face is lined, your hair is grey.

RUTH
It's gradually got so.

FREDERIC
Faithless woman, to deceive me,
I who trusted so!

RUTH
Master, master, do not leave me!
Hear me, ere you go!
My love without reflecting,

Oh, do not be rejecting!
Take a maiden tender, her affection raw and green,
At very highest rating,
Has been accumulating
Summers seventeen, summers seventeen.
Don't, beloved master,
Crush me with disaster.
What is such a dower to the dower I have here?
My love unabating
Has been accumulating
Forty-seven year—forty-seven year!

ENSEMBLE

RUTH	**FREDERIC**
Don't, beloved master,	Yes, your former master
Crush me with disaster.	Saves you from disaster.
What is such a dower to the	Your love would be uncomfortably
dower I have here	fervid, it is clear
My love unabating	If, as you are stating
Has been accumulating	It's been accumulating
Forty-seven year, forty-seven year!	Forty-seven year—forty-seven year!
	Faithless woman to deceive me, I who trusted so!
Master, master, do not leave	Faithless woman to deceive me, I
me, hear me, ere I go!	who trusted so!

RECITATIVE—**FREDERIC**
What shall I do? Before these gentle maidens
I dare not show in this alarming costume!
No, no, I must remain in close concealment
Until I can appear in decent clothing!

(Hides in cave as they enter climbing over the rocks and through arched rock)

GIRLS
Climbing over rocky mountain,
Skipping rivulet and fountain,
Passing where the willows quiver,
Passing where the willows quiver
By the ever-rolling river,
Swollen with the summer rain, the summer rain
Threading long and leafy mazes
Dotted with unnumbered daisies,
Dotted, dotted with unnumbered daisies,
Scaling rough and rugged passes,
Climb the hardy little lasses,
Till the bright sea-shore they gain;
Scaling rough and rugged passes,

Climb the hardy little lasses,
Till the bright sea-shore they gain!

EDITH
Let us gaily tread the measure,
Make the most of fleeting leisure,
Hail it as a true ally,
Though it perish by-and-by.

GIRLS
Hail it as a true ally,
Though it perish by-and-by.

EDITH
Every moment brings a treasure
Of its own especial pleasure;
Though the moments quickly die,
Greet them gaily as they fly,
Greet them gaily as they fly.

GIRLS
Though the moments quickly die,
Greet them gaily as they fly.

KATE
Far away from toil and care,
Revelling in fresh sea-air,
Here we live and reign alone
In a world that's all our own.
Here, in this our rocky den,
Far away from mortal men,
We'll be queens, and make decrees—
They may honour them who please.

GIRLS
We'll be queens, and make decrees—
They may honour them who please.
Let us gaily tread the measure, etc.

KATE
What a picturesque spot! I wonder where we are!

EDITH
And I wonder where Papa is. We have left him ever so far behind.

ISABEL
Oh, he will be here presently! Remember poor Papa is not as young as we are, and we came over a rather difficult country.

KATE
But how thoroughly delightful it is to be so entirely alone! Why, in all probability we are the first human beings who ever set foot on this enchanting spot.

ISABEL
Except the mermaids—it's the very place for mermaids.

KATE
Who are only human beings down to the waist—

EDITH
And who can't be said strictly to set foot anywhere.
Tails they may, but feet they cannot.

KATE
But what shall we do until Papa and the servants arrive with the luncheon?

EDITH
We are quite alone, and the sea is as smooth as glass.
Suppose we take off our shoes and stockings and paddle?

ALL
Yes, yes! The very thing!

(They prepare to carry, out the suggestion. They have all taken off one shoe, when FREDERIC comes forward from cave.)

FREDERIC (recitative)
Stop, ladies, pray!

GIRLS (Hopping on one foot)
A man!

FREDERIC
I had intended
Not to intrude myself upon your notice
In this effective but alarming costume;
But under these peculiar circumstances,
It is my bounden duty to inform you
That your proceedings will not be unwitnessed!

EDITH
But who are you, sir? Speak!

(ALL hopping)

FREDERIC

I am a pirate!

GIRLS (recoiling, hopping)
A pirate! Horror!

FREDERIC
Ladies, do not shun me!
This evening I renounce my vile profession;
And, to that end, O pure and peerless maidens!
Oh, blushing buds of ever-blooming beauty!
I, sore at heart, implore your kind assistance.

EDITH
How pitiful his tale!

KATE
How rare his beauty

GIRLS
How pitiful his tale! How rare his beauty!

SONG—**FREDERIC**
Oh, is there not one maiden breast
Which does not feel the moral beauty
Of making worldly interest
Subordinate to sense of duty?

Who would not give up willingly
All matrimonial ambition,
To rescue such a one as I
From his unfortunate position?
From his position,
To rescue such an one as I
From his unfortunate position?

GIRLS
Alas! there's not one maiden breast
Which seems to feel the moral beauty
Of making worldly interest
Subordinate to sense of duty!

FREDERIC
Oh, is there not one maiden here
Whose homely face and bad complexion
Have caused all hope to disappear
Of ever winning man's affection?
Of such a one, if such there be,
I swear by Heaven's arch above you,

If you will cast your eyes on me,
However plain you be, I'll love you,
However plain you be,
If you will cast your eyes on me,
However plain you be I'll love you,
I'll love you, I'll love, I'll love you!

GIRLS
Alas! there's not one maiden here
Whose homely face and bad complexion
Have caused all hope to disappear
Of ever winning man's affection!

FREDERIC (in despair)
Not one?

GIRLS
No, no— not one!

FREDERIC
Not one?

GIRLS
No, no!

MABEL (enters through arch)
Yes, one!
Yes, one!

GIRLS
'Tis Mabel!

MABEL
Yes, 'tis Mabel!

RECITATIVE—**MABEL**
Oh, sisters, deaf to pity's name,
For shame!
It's true that he has gone astray,
But pray
Is that a reason good and true
Why you
Should all be deaf to pity's name?

GIRLS
(aside)The question is, had he not been
A thing of beauty,
Would she be swayed by quite as keen

A sense of duty?

MABEL
For shame, for shame, for shame!

SONG—**MABEL**

MABEL
Poor wand'ring one!
Though thou hast surely strayed,
Take heart of grace,
Thy steps retrace,
Poor wand'ring one!
Poor wand'ring one!
If such poor love as mine
Can help thee find
True peace of mind-
Why, take it, it is thine!

GIRLS
Take heart, no danger low'rs;
Take any heart but ours!

MABEL
Take heart, fair days will shine;
Take any heart—take mine!

GIRLS
Take heart; no danger low'rs;
Take any heart-but ours!

MABEL
Take heart, fair days will shine;
Take any heart—take mine!
Poor wand'ring one!, etc.

(MABEL and FREDERIC go to mouth of cave and converse. EDITH beckons her sisters, who form a semi-circle around her.)

EDITH
What ought we to do,
Gentle sisters, say?
Propriety, we know,
Says we ought to stay;
While sympathy exclaims,
"Free them from your tether—
Play at other games—
Leave them here together."

KATE
Her case may, any day,
Be yours, my dear, or mine.
Let her make her hay
While the sun doth shine.
Let us compromise
(Our hearts are not of leather):
Let us shut our eyes
And talk about the weather.

GIRLS
Yes, yes, let's talk about the weather.

Chattering CHORUS

How beautifully blue the sky,
The glass is rising very high,
Continue fine I hope it may,
And yet it rained but yesterday.
To-morrow it may pour again
(I hear the country wants some rain),
Yet people say, I know not why,
That we shall have a warm July.
To-morrow it may pour again
(I hear the country wants some rain),
Yet people say, I know not why,
That we shall have a warm July.

Enter MABEL and FREDERIC

During MABEL's solo the GIRLS continue chatter pianissimo, but listening eagerly all the time.

SOLO—**MABEL**

Did ever maiden wake
From dream of homely duty,
To find her daylight break
With such exceeding beauty?
Did ever maiden close
Her eyes on waking sadness,
To dream of such exceeding gladness?

FREDERIC
Ah, yes! ah, yes! this is exceeding gladness

GIRLS
How beautifully blue the sky, etc.

SOLO—**FREDERIC**
During this, GIRLS continue their chatter pianissimo as before, but listening intently all the time.

Did ever pirate roll
His soul in guilty dreaming,
And wake to find that soul
With peace and virtue beaming?

ENSEMBLE

FREDERIC	**MABEL**	**GIRLS**
Did ever pirate loathed Forsake his hideous mission To find himself betrothed To lady of position?	Did ever maiden wake From dream of homely duty, To find her daylight break With such exceeding beauty?	How beautifully blue the sky, etc.

RECIT—**FREDERIC**

Stay, we must not lose our senses;
Men who stick at no offences
Will anon be here!
Piracy their dreadful trade is;
Pray you, get you hence, young ladies,
While the coast is clear

(FREDERIC and MABEL retire)

GIRLS
No, we must not lose our senses,
If they stick at no offences
We should not be here!
Piracy their dreadful trade is—
Nice companions for young ladies!
Let us disap—.

(During this chorus the PIRATES have entered stealthily, and formed in a semicircle behind the GIRLS. As the GIRLS move to go off, each PIRATE seizes a GIRL. KING seizes EDITH and ISABEL, SAMUEL seizes KATE.)

GIRLS
Too late!

PIRATES
Ha, ha!

GIRLS
Too late!

PIRATES
Ho, ho!
Ha, ha, ha, ha! Ho, ho, ho, ho!

ENSEMBLE

(PIRATES pass in front of GIRLS!)   (GIRLS pass in front of PIRATES.)

PIRATES	**GIRLS**
Here's a first-rate opportunity	We have missed our opportunity
To get married with impunity,	Of escaping with impunity;
And indulge in the felicity	So farewell to the felicity
Of unbounded domesticity.	Of our maiden domesticity!
You shall quickly be	We shall quickly be
parsonified,	parsonified,
Conjugally matrimonified,	Conjugally matrimonified,
By a doctor of divinity	By a doctor of divinity,
Who is located in this	Who is located in this
vicinity.	vicinity.
By a doctor of divinity,	By a doctor of divinity,
Who resides in this vicinity,	Who resides in this vicinity,
By a doctor, a doctor, a doctor	By a doctor, a doctor, a doctor
of divinity, of divinity.	of divinity, of divinity.

RECITATIVE

MABEL (coming forward)
Hold, monsters! Ere your pirate caravanserai
Proceed, against our will, to wed us all,
Just bear in mind that we are Wards in Chancery,
And father is a Major-General!

SAMUEL (cowed)
We'd better pause, or danger may befall,
Their father is a Major-General.

GIRLS
Yes, yes; he is a Major-General!

(The MAJOR-GENERAL has entered unnoticed, on the rock)

GENERAL
Yes, yes, I am a Major-General!

SAMUEL
For he is a Major-General!

ALL
He is! Hurrah for the Major-General!

GENERAL
And it is, it is a glorious thing
To be a Major-General!

ALL
It is! Hurrah for the Major-General!
Hurrah for the Major-General!

SONG—**MAJOR-GENERAL**
I am the very model of a modern Major-General,
I've information vegetable, animal, and mineral,
I know the kings of England, and I quote the fights historical
From Marathon to Waterloo, in order categorical;
I'm very well acquainted, too, with matters mathematical,
I understand equations, both the simple and quadratical,
About binomial theorem I'm teeming with a lot o' news,
With many cheerful facts about the square of the hypotenuse.

ALL
With many cheerful facts, etc.

GENERAL
I'm very good at integral and differential calculus;
I know the scientific names of beings animalculous:
In short, in matters vegetable, animal, and mineral,
I am the very model of a modern Major-General.

ALL
In short, in matters vegetable, animal, and mineral,
He is the very model of a modern Major-General.

GENERA
I know our mythic history, King Arthur's and Sir Caradoc's;
I answer hard acrostics, I've a pretty taste for paradox,
I quote in elegiacs all the crimes of Heliogabalus,
In conics I can floor peculiarities parabolous;
I can tell undoubted Raphaels from Gerard Dows and Zoffanies,
I know the croaking chorus from the Frogs of Aristophanes!
Then I can hum a fugue of which I've heard the music's din afore,
And whistle all the airs from that infernal nonsense Pinafore.

ALL

And whistle all the airs, etc.

GENERAL
Then I can write a washing bill in Babylonic cuneiform,
And tell you ev'ry detail of Caractacus's uniform:
In short, in matters vegetable, animal, and mineral,
I am the very model of a modern Major-General.

ALL
In short, in matters vegetable, animal, and mineral,
He is the very model of a modern Major-General.

GENERAL
In fact, when I know what is meant by "mamelon" and "ravelin",
When I can tell at sight a Mauser rifle from a javelin,
When such affairs as sorties and surprises I'm more wary at,
And when I know precisely what is meant by "commissariat",
When I have learnt what progress has been made in modern gunnery,
When I know more of tactics than a novice in a nunnery—
In short, when I've a smattering of elemental strategy,
You'll say a better Major-General has never sat a gee.

ALL
You'll say a better Major-General, etc.

GENERAL
For my military knowledge, though I'm plucky and adventury,
Has only been brought down to the beginning of the century;
But still, in matters vegetable, animal, and mineral,
I am the very model of a modern Major-General.

ALL
But still, in matters vegetable, animal, and mineral,
He is the very model of a modern Major-General.

GENERAL
And now that I've introduced myself, I should like to have some idea of what's going on.

KATE
Oh, Papa— we—

SAMUEL
Permit me, I'll explain in two words: we propose to marry your daughters.

GENERAL
Dear me!

GIRLS

Against our wills, Papa—against our wills!

GENERAL
Oh, but you mustn't do that! May I ask—this is a picturesque uniform, but I'm not familiar with it. What are you?

KING
We are all single gentlemen.

GENERAL
Yes, I gathered that. Anything else?

KING
No, nothing else.

EDITH
Papa, don't believe them; they are pirates—the famous Pirates of Penzance!

GENERAL
The Pirates of Penzance! I have often heard of them.

MABEL
All except this gentleman (indicating FREDERIC), who was a pirate once, but who is out of his indentures to-day, and who means to lead a blameless life evermore.

GENERAL
But wait a bit. I object to pirates as sons-in-law.

KING
We object to major-generals as fathers-in-law. But we waive that point. We do not press it. We look over it.

GENERAL (aside)
Hah! an idea! (aloud) And do you mean to say that you would deliberately rob me of these, the sole remaining props of my old age, and leave me to go through the remainder of my life unfriended, unprotected, and alone?

KING
Well, yes, that's the idea.

GENERAL
Tell me, have you ever known what it is to be an orphan?

PIRATES (disgusted)
Oh, dash it all!

KING
Here we are again!

GENERAL
I ask you, have you ever known what it is to be an orphan?

KING
Often!

GENERAL
Yes, orphan. Have you ever known what it is to be one?

KING
I say, often.

ALL (disgusted)
Often, often, often.

(Turning away)

GENERAL
I don't think we quite understand one another. I ask you, have you ever known what it is to be an orphan, and you say "orphan". As I understand you, you are merely repeating the word "orphan" to show that you understand me.

KING
I didn't repeat the word often.

GENERAL
Pardon me, you did indeed.

KING
I only repeated it once.

GENERAL
True, but you repeated it.

KING
But not often.

GENERAL
Stop! I think I see where we are getting confused. When you said "orphan", did you mean "orphan", a person who has lost his parents, or "often", frequently?

KING
Ah! I beg pardon— I see what you mean — frequently.

GENERAL
Ah! you said "often", frequently.

KING
No, only once.

GENERAL (irritated)
Exactly— you said "often", frequently, only once.

FINALE OF ACT I

GENERAL
Oh, men of dark and dismal fate,
Forgo your cruel employ,
Have pity on my lonely state,
I am an orphan boy!

KING/SAMUEL
An orphan boy?

GENERAL
An orphan boy!

PIRATES
How sad, an orphan boy.

GENERAL
These children whom you see
Are all that I can call my own!

PIRATES
Poor fellow!

GENERAL
Take them away from me,
And I shall be indeed alone.

PIRATES
 Poor fellow!

GENERAL
If pity you can feel,
Leave me my sole remaining joy—
See, at your feet they kneel;
Your hearts you cannot steel
Against the sad, sad tale of the lonely orphan boy!

PIRATES
(sobbing) Poor fellow!
See at our feet they kneel;
Our hearts we cannot steel

Against the sad, sad tale of the lonely orphan boy!

SAMUEL
The orphan boy!

KING
The orphan boy!
See at our feet they kneel;
Our hearts we cannot steel
Against the tale of the lonely orphan boy!

PIRATES
Poor fellow!

ENSEMBLE

GENERAL (aside)
I'm telling a terrible story
But it doesn't diminish
my glory;
For they would have
taken my daughters
Over the billowy waters,
daughters
Over the billowy waters,
If I hadn't, in elegant
diction,
Indulged in an innocent
fiction,
Which is not in the same
category
As a regular terrible
terrible story.

GIRLS (aside)
He is telling a terrible story
Which will tend to
diminish his
glory;
Though they would have
taken his
That ever were
these
It is easy, in elegant
diction.
To call it an innocent
fiction,
But it comes in the same
category
As telling a regular
terrible story.

PIRATES (aside)
If he's telling a terrible story
He shall die by a death
that is gory
Yes, one of the
cruellest
slaughters
known in
waters;
It is easy, in elegant
diction,
To call it an innocent
fiction
But it comes in the same
category
As telling a regular story.

KING
Although our dark career
Sometimes involves the crime of stealing,
We rather think that we're
Not altogether void of feeling.
Although we live by strife,
We're always sorry to begin it,
For what, we ask, is life
Without a touch of Poetry in it?

(ALL kneel)

ALL
Hail, Poetry, thou heav'n-born maid!

Thou gildest e'en the pirate's trade.
Hail, flowing fount of sentiment!
All hail, all hail, divine emollient!

(ALL rise)

KING
You may go, for you're at liberty, our pirate rules protect you,
And honorary members of our band we do elect you!

SAMUEL
For he is an orphan boy!

CHORUS
He is! Hurrah for the orphan boy!

GENERAL
And it sometimes is a useful thing
To be an orphan boy.

CHORUS
It is! Hurrah for the orphan boy!
Hurrah for the orphan boy!

ENSEMBLE
Oh, happy day, with joyous glee
They will away and married be!
Should it befall auspiciously,
Her (Our) sisters all will bridesmaids be!

(RUTH enters and comes down to FREDERIC)

RUTH
Oh, master, hear one word, I do implore you!
Remember Ruth, your Ruth, who kneels before you!

PIRATES
Yes, yes, remember Ruth, who kneels before you!

FREDERIC
Away, you did deceive me!

PIRATES (Threatening RUTH)
Away, you did deceive him!

RUTH
Oh, do not leave me!

PIRATES
Oh, do not leave her!

FREDERIC
Away, you grieve me!

PIRATES
Away, you grieve him!

FREDERIC
I wish you'd leave me!

(FREDERIC casts RUTH from him)

PIRATES
We wish you'd leave him!

ENSEMBLE

MEN	**WOMEN**
Pray observe the magnanimity	Pray observe the magnanimity
We display to lace and dimity!	They display to lace and dimity!
Never was such opportunity	Never was such opportunity
To get married with impunity,	To get married with impunity,
But we give up the felicity	But they give up the felicity
Of unbounded domesticity,	Of unbounded domesticity,
Though a doctor of divinity	Though a doctor of divinity
Is located in this vicinity.	Is located in this vicinity.

(GIRLS and MAJOR-GENERAL go up rocks, while PIRATES indulge in a wild dance of delight on stage. The MAJOR-GENERAL produces a British flag, and the PIRATE KING, in arched rock, produces a black flag with skull and crossbones.

Enter RUTH, who makes a final appeal to FREDERIC, who casts her from him.)

END OF ACT I

ACT II

(Scene.-A ruined chapel by moonlight. Aisles C., R. and L., divided by pillars and arches, ruined Gothic windows at back. MAJOR-GENERAL STANLEY discovered seated R.C. pensively, surrounded by his daughters.)

CHORUS

Oh, dry the glist'ning tear
That dews that martial cheek,
Thy loving children hear,
In them thy comfort seek.
With sympathetic care
Their arms around thee creep,
For oh, they cannot bear
To see their father weep!

(Enter MABEL)

SOLO—**MABEL**

Dear father, why leave your bed
At this untimely hour,
When happy daylight is dead,
And darksome dangers low'r?
See, heav'n has lit her lamp,
The midnight hour is past,
And the chilly night-air is damp,
And the dews are falling fast!
Dear father, why leave your bed
When happy daylight is dead?

GIRLS
Oh, dry the glist'ning tear, etc.

(FREDERIC enters)

MABEL
Oh, Frederic, cannot you, in the calm excellence of your wisdom, reconcile it with your conscience to say something that will relieve my father's sorrow?

FREDERIC
I will try, dear Mabel. But why does he sit, night after night, in this draughty old ruin?

GENERAL
Why do I sit here? To escape from the pirates' clutches, I described myself as an orphan; and, heaven help me, I am no orphan! I come here to humble myself before the tombs of my ancestors, and to implore their pardon for having brought dishonour on the family escutcheon.

FREDERIC
But you forget, sir, you only bought the property a year ago, and the stucco on your baronial castle is scarcely dry.

GENERAL
Frederic, in this chapel are ancestors: you cannot deny that. With the estate, I bought the chapel and its

contents. I don't know whose ancestors they were, but I know whose ancestors they are, and I shudder to think that their descendant by purchase (if I may so describe myself) should have brought disgrace upon what, I have no doubt, was an unstained escutcheon.

FREDERIC
Be comforted. Had you not acted as you did, these reckless men would assuredly have called in the nearest clergyman, and have married your large family on the spot.

GENERAL
I thank you for your proffered solace, but it is unavailing. I assure you, Frederic, that such is the anguish and remorse I feel at the abominable falsehood by which I escaped these easily deluded pirates, that I would go to their simple-minded chief this very night and confess all, did I not fear that the consequences would be most disastrous to myself. At what time does your expedition march against these scoundrels?

FREDERIC
At eleven, and before midnight I hope to have atoned for my involuntary association with the pestilent scourges by sweeping them from the face of the earth—and then, dear Mabel, you will be mine!

GENERAL
Are your devoted followers at hand?

FREDERIC
They are, they only wait my orders.

RECITATIVE—**GENERAL**
Then, Frederic, let your escort lion-hearted
Be summoned to receive a gen'ral's blessing,
Ere they depart upon their dread adventure.

FREDERIC
Dear, sir, they come.

(Enter POLICE, marching in single file. They form in line, facing audience.)

SONG—**SERGEANT**
When the foeman bares his steel,
Tarantara! tarantara!
We uncomfortable feel,
Tarantara!
And we find the wisest thing,
Tarantara! tarantara!
Is to slap our chests and sing,
Tarantara!
For when threatened with -meutes,
Tarantara! tarantara!
And your heart is in your boots,
Tarantara!

There is nothing brings it round
Like the trumpet's martial sound,
Like the trumpet's martial sound
Tarantara! tarantara!, etc.

MABEL
Go, ye heroes, go to glory,
Though you die in combat gory,
Ye shall live in song and story.
Go to immortality!
Go to death, and go to slaughter;
Die, and every Cornish daughter
With her tears your grave shall water.
Go, ye heroes, go and die!

GIRLS
Go, ye heroes, go and die! Go, ye heroes, go and die!

POLICE
Though to us it's evident,
Tarantara! tarantara!
These attentions are well meant,
Tarantara!
Such expressions don't appear,
Tarantara! tarantara!
Calculated men to cheer
Tarantara!
Who are going to meet their fate
In a highly nervous state.
Tarantara! tarantara! tarantara!
Still to us it's evident
These attentions are well meant.
Tarantara! tarantara! tarantara!

EDITH
Go and do your best endeavour,
And before all links we sever,
We will say farewell for-ever.
Go to glory and the grave!

GIRLS
For your foes are fierce and ruthless,
False, unmerciful, and truthless;
Young and tender, old and toothless,
All in vain their mercy crave.

SERGEANT
We observe too great a stress,

On the risks that on us press,
And of reference a lack
To our chance of coming back.
Still, perhaps it would be wise
Not to carp or criticise,
For it's very evident
These attentions are well meant.

POLICE
Yes, it's very evident
These attentions are well meant,
Evident, yes, well meant, evident
Ah, yes, well meant!

ENSEMBLE

CHORUS OF ALL BUT POLICE	**CHORUS OF POLICE**
Go and do your best endeavour,	Such expressions don't appear,
And before all links we sever	Tarantara, tarantara!
We will say farewell for ever.	Calculated men to cheer,
Go to glory and the grave!	Tarantara!
For your foes and fierce and ruthless	Who are going to their fate, Tarantara, tarantara!
False, unmerciful, and truthless	In a highly nervous state—Tarantara!
Young and tender, old and toothless	We observe too great a stress, Tarantara, tarantara!
All in vain their mercy crave.	On the risks that on us press,
	And of reference a lack, Tarantara, tarantara!
	To our chance of coming back, Tarantara!

GENERAL
Away, away!

POLICE (without moving)
Yes, yes, we go.

GENERAL
These pirates slay.

POLICE
Tarantara!

GENERAL
Then do not stay.

POLICE
Tarantara!

GENERAL
Then why this delay?

POLICE
All right, we go.

ALL
Yes, forward on the foe!
Yes, forward on the foe!

GENERAL
Yes, but you don't go!

POLICE
We go, we go

ALL
Yes, forward on the foe!
Yes, forward on the foe!

GENERAL
Yes, but you don't go!

POLICE
We go, we go

ALL
At last they go!
At last they really go!

(Exeunt POLICE. MABEL tears herself from FREDERIC and exits, followed by her sisters, consoling her. The MAJOR-GENERAL and others follow the POLICE off. FREDERIC remains alone.)

RECITATIVE-**FREDERIC**

Now for the pirates' lair! Oh, joy unbounded!
Oh, sweet relief! Oh, rapture unexampled!
At last I may atone, in some slight measure,
For the repeated acts of theft and pillage
Which, at a sense of duty's stern dictation,
I, circumstance's victim, have been guilty!

(PIRATE KING and RUTH appear at the window, armed.)

KING
Young Frederic!

(Covering him with pistol)

FREDERIC
Who calls?

KING
Your late commander!

RUTH
And I, your little Ruth!

(Covering him with pistol)

FREDERIC
Oh, mad intruders,
How dare ye face me? Know ye not, oh rash ones,
That I have doomed you to extermination?

(KING and RUTH hold a pistol to each ear)

KING
Have mercy on us! hear us, ere you slaughter!

FREDERIC
I do not think I ought to listen to you.
Yet, mercy should alloy our stern resentment,
And so I will be merciful— say on!

TRIO—**RUTH**, **KING**, and **FREDERIC**

RUTH
When you had left our pirate fold,
We tried to raise our spirits faint,
According to our custom old,
With quips and quibbles quaint.
But all in vain the quips we heard,
We lay and sobbed upon the rocks,
Until to somebody occurred
A startling paradox.

FREDERIC
A paradox?

KING (laughing)
A paradox!

RUTH
A most ingenious paradox!
We've quips and quibbles heard in flocks,
But none to beat this paradox!
A paradox, a paradox,
A most ingenious paradox!

Ha! ha! ha! ha! Ha! ha! ha! ha!

KING
We knew your taste for curious quips,
For cranks and contradictions queer;
And with the laughter on our lips,
We wished you there to hear.
We said, "If we could tell it him,
How Frederic would the joke enjoy!"
And so we've risked both life and limb
To tell it to our boy.

FREDERIC
(interested)That paradox? That paradox?

KING and **RUTH**
(laughing)That most ingenious paradox!
We've quips and quibbles heard in flocks,
But none to beat this paradox!
A paradox, a paradox,
A most ingenious paradox!
Ha! ha! ha! ha! Ho! ho! ho! ho!

CHANT—**KING**

For some ridiculous reason, to which, however, I've no desire to be disloyal,
Some person in authority, I don't know who, very likely the Astronomer Royal,
Has decided that, although for such a beastly month as February,
twenty-eight days as a rule are plenty,
One year in every four his days shall be reckoned as nine and-twenty.
Through some singular coincidence— I shouldn't be surprised if
it were owing to the agency of an ill-natured fairy—
You are the victim of this clumsy arrangement, having been born
in leap-year, on the twenty-ninth of February;
And so, by a simple arithmetical process, you'll easily discover,
That though you've lived twenty-one years, yet, if we go by
birthdays, you're only five and a little bit over!

RUTH
Ha! ha! ha! ha!

KING
Ho! ho! ho! ho!

FREDERIC
Dear me!
Let's see! (counting on fingers)
Yes, yes; with yours my figures do agree!

ALL
Ha! ha! ha! ho! ho! ho! ho!

FREDERIC (more amused than any)
How quaint the ways of Paradox!
At common sense she gaily mocks!
Though counting in the usual way,
Years twenty-one I've been alive,
Yet, reck'ning by my natal day,
Yet, reck'ning by my natal day,
I am a little boy of five!

RUTH/KING
He is a little boy of five!
Ha! ha! ha! ha! ha! ha! ha! ha!

ALL
A paradox, a paradox,
A most ingenious paradox!
Ha! ha! ha! ha! ha! ha! ha! ha!, etc.

(RUTH and KING throw themselves back on seats, exhausted with laughter)

FREDERIC
Upon my word, this is most curious— most absurdly whimsical. Five-and-a-quarter! No one would think it to look at me!

RUTH
You are glad now, I'll be bound, that you spared us. You would never have forgiven yourself when you discovered that you had killed two of your comrades.

FREDERIC
My comrades?

KING (rises)
I'm afraid you don't appreciate the delicacy of your position: You were apprenticed to us—

FREDERIC
Until I reached my twenty-first year.

KING
No, until you reached your twenty-first birthday (producing document), and, going by birthdays, you are as yet only five-and-a-quarter.

FREDERIC
You don't mean to say you are going to hold me to that?

KING
No, we merely remind you of the fact, and leave the rest to your sense of duty.

RUTH
Your sense of duty!

FREDERIC (wildly)
Don't put it on that footing! As I was merciful to you just now, be merciful to me! I implore you not to insist on the letter of your bond just as the cup of happiness is at my lips!

RUTH
We insist on nothing; we content ourselves with pointing out to you your duty.

KING
Your duty!

FREDERIC (after a pause)
Well, you have appealed to my sense of duty, and my duty is only too clear. I abhor your infamous calling; I shudder at the thought that I have ever been mixed up with it; but duty is before all—at any price I will do my duty.

KING
Bravely spoken! Come, you are one of us once more.

FREDERIC
Lead on, I follow. (Suddenly) Oh, horror!

KING/RUTH
What is the matter?

FREDERIC
Ought I to tell you? No, no, I cannot do it; and yet, as one of your band—

KING
Speak out, I charge you by that sense of conscientiousness to which we have never yet appealed in vain.

FREDERIC
General Stanley, the father of my Mabel—

KING/RUTH
Yes, yes!

FREDERIC
He escaped from you on the plea that he was an orphan?

KING
He did.

FREDERIC
It breaks my heart to betray the honoured father of the girl I adore, but as your apprentice I have no alternative. It is my duty to tell you that General Stanley is no orphan!

KING/RUTH
What!

FREDERIC
More than that, he never was one!

KING
Am I to understand that, to save his contemptible life, he dared to practice on our credulous simplicity?

(FREDERIC nods as he weeps) Our revenge shall be swift and terrible. We will go and collect our band and attack Tremorden Castle this very night.

FREDERIC
But stay—

KING
Not a word! He is doomed!

TRIO – KING, RUTH and FREDERIC

KING and RUTH
Away, away! my heart's on fire
I burn, this base deception to do to repay
This very night my vengeance dire
Shall glut itself in gore.
Away, away!

FREDERIC
Away, away! ere I expire—
I find my duty hard Today!
My heart is filled with anguish dire,
It strikes me to the core.
Away, away!

KING
With falsehood foul
He tricked us of our brides.
Let vengeance howl;
The Pirate so decides.
Our nature stern
He softened with his lies,
And, in return,
To-night the traitor dies.

ALL
Yes, yes! to-night the traitor dies!
Yes, yes! to-night the traitor dies!

RUTH
To-night he dies!

KING
Yes, or early to-morrow.

FREDERIC
His girls likewise?

RUTH
They will welter in sorrow.

KING
The one soft spot

RUTH
In their natures they cherish—

FREDERIC
And all who plot

KING
To abuse it shall perish!

ALL
To-night he dies, etc.

(Exeunt KING and RUTH. FREDERIC throws himself on a stone in blank despair. Enter MABEL.)

RECITATIVE—**MABEL**

All is prepared, your gallant crew await you.
My Frederic in tears? It cannot be
That lion-heart quails at the coming conflict?

FREDERIC
No, Mabel, no.
A terrible disclosure
Has just been made.
Mabel, my dearly-loved one,
I bound myself to serve the pirate captain
Until I reached my one-and-twentieth birthday—

MABEL
But you are twenty-one?

FREDERIC
I've just discovered
That I was born in leap-year, and that birthday
Will not be reached by me till nineteen forty!

MABEL
Oh, horrible! catastrophe appalling!

FREDERIC
And so, farewell!

MABEL
No, no!
Ah, Frederic, hear me.

DUET—**MABEL** and **FREDERIC**

MABEL
Stay, Fred'ric, stay!
They have no legal claim,
No shadow of a shame
Will fall upon thy name.
Stay, Frederic, stay!

FREDERIC
Nay, Mabel, nay!
To-night I quit these walls,
The thought my soul appalls,
But when stern Duty calls,
I must obey.

MABEL
Stay, Fred'ric, stay!

FREDERIC
Nay, Mabel, nay!

MABEL
They have no claim—

FREDERIC
But Duty's name.
The thought my soul appalls,
But when stern Duty calls,

MABEL
Stay, Fred'ric, stay!

FREDERIC
I must obey.

BALLAD—**MABEL**
Ah, leave me not to pine

Alone and desolate;
No fate seemed fair as mine,
No happiness so great!
And Nature, day by day,
Has sung in accents clear
This joyous roundelay,
"He loves thee— he is here.
Fa-la, la-la,
Fa-la, la-la.
He loves thee— he is here.
Fa-la, la-la, Fa-la."

FREDERIC
Ah, must I leave thee here
In endless night to dream,
Where joy is dark and drear,
And sorrow all supreme—
Where nature, day by day,
Will sing, in altered tone,
This weary roundelay,
"He loves thee— he is gone.
Fa-la, la-la,
Fa-la, la-la.
He loves thee— he is gone.
Fa-la, la-la, Fa-la."

FREDERIC
In 1940 I of age shall be,
I'll then return, and claim you—I declare it!

MABEL
It seems so long!

FREDERIC
Swear that, till then, you will be true to me.

MABEL
Yes, I'll be strong!
By all the Stanleys dead and gone, I swear it!

ENSEMBLE
Oh, here is love, and here is truth,
And here is food for joyous laughter:
He (she) will be faithful to his (her) sooth
Till we are wed, and even after.
Oh, here is love, etc.

(FREDERIC rushes to window and leaps out)

MABEL (almost fainting)
No, I am brave! Oh, family descent,
How great thy charm, thy sway how excellent!
Come one and all, undaunted men in blue,
A crisis, now, affairs are coming to!

(Enter POLICE, marching in single file)

SERGEANT
Though in body and in mind

POLICE
Tarantara! tarantara!

SERGEANT
We are timidly inclined,

POLICE
Tarantara!

SERGEANT
And anything but blind

POLICE
Tarantara! tarantara!

SERGEANT
To the danger that's behind,

POLICE
Tarantara!

SERGEANT
Yet, when the danger's near,

POLICE
Tarantara! tarantara!

SERGEANT
 We manage to appear
POLICE
Tarantara!

SERGEANT
As insensible to fear
As anybody here,
As anybody here.

POLICE
Tarantara! tarantara!, etc.

MABEL
Sergeant, approach! Young Frederic was to have led you to death and glory.

POLICE
That is not a pleasant way of putting it.

MABEL
No matter; he will not so lead you, for he has allied himself once more with his old associates.

POLICE
He has acted shamefully!

MABEL
You speak falsely. You know nothing about it. He has acted nobly.

POLICE
He has acted nobly!

MABEL
Dearly as I loved him before, his heroic sacrifice to his sense of duty has endeared him to me tenfold; but if it was his duty to constitute himself my foe, it is likewise my duty to regard him in that light. He has done his duty. I will do mine. Go ye and do yours.

(Exit MABEL)

POLICE
Right oh!

SERGEANT
This is perplexing.

POLICE
We cannot understand it at all.

SERGEANT
Still, as he is actuated by a sense of duty—

POLICE
That makes a difference, of course. At the same time, we repeat, we cannot understand it at all.

SERGEANT
No matter. Our course is clear: we must do our best to capture these pirates alone. It is most distressing to us to be the agents whereby our erring fellow-creatures are deprived of that liberty which is so dear to us all— but we should have thought of that before we joined the force.

POLICE
We should!

SERGEANT
It is too late now!

POLICE
It is!

SOLO AND **CHORUS**

SERGEANT
When a felon's not engaged in his employment

POLICE
His employment

SERGEANT
Or maturing his felonious little plans,

POLICE
Little plans,

SERGEANT
His capacity for innocent enjoyment

POLICE
'Cent enjoyment

SERGEANT
Is just as great as any honest man's.

POLICE
Honest man's.

SERGEANT
Our feelings we with difficulty smother

POLICE
'Culty smother

SERGEANT
When constabulary duty's to be done.

POLICE
To be done.

SERGEANT
Ah, take one consideration with another,

POLICE
With another,

SERGEANT
A policeman's lot is not a happy one.

ALL
Ah, when constabulary duty's to be done, to be done,
A policeman's lot is not a happy one, happy one.

SERGEANT
When the enterprising burglar's not a-burgling

POLICE
Not a-burgling

SERGEANT
When the cut-throat isn't occupied in crime,

POLICE
'Pied in crime,

SERGEANT
He loves to hear the little brook a-gurgling

POLICE
Brook a-gurgling

SERGEANT
And listen to the merry village chime.

POLICE
Village chime.

SERGEANT
When the coster's finished jumping on his mother,

POLICE
On his mother,

SERGEANT
He loves to lie a-basking in the sun.

POLICE
In the sun.

SERGEANT
Ah, take one consideration with another,

POLICE
With another,

SERGEANT
A policeman's lot is not a happy one.

ALL
Ah, when constabulary duty's to be done, to be done,
A policeman's lot is not a happy one, happy one.

(CHORUS OFPIRATES without, in the distance)

A rollicking band of pirates we,
Who, tired of tossing on the sea,
Are trying their hand at a burglaree,
With weapons grim and gory.

SERGEANT
Hush, hush! I hear them on the manor poaching,
With stealthy step the pirates are approaching.

(CHORUS OF PIRATES, resumed nearer.)

We are not coming for plate or gold;
A story General Stanley's told;
We seek a penalty fifty-fold,
For General Stanley's story.

POLICE
They seek a penalty

PIRATES
Fifty-fold!
We seek a penalty

POLICE
Fifty-fold!

ALL
They/We seek a penalty fifty-fold,
For General Stanley's story.

SERGEANT
They come in force, with stealthy stride,

Our obvious course is now—to hide.

POLICE
Tarantara! Tarantara! etc.

(POLICE conceal themselves in aisle. As they do so, the PIRATES, with RUTH and FREDERIC, are seen appearing at ruined window. They enter cautiously, and come down stage on tiptoe. SAMUEL is laden with burglarious tools and pistols, etc.)

CHORUS—**PIRATES** (very loud)
With cat-like tread,
Upon our prey we steal;
In silence dread,
Our cautious way we feel.
No sound at all!
We never speak a word;
A fly's foot-fall
Would be distinctly heard—

POLICE (softly)
Tarantara, tarantara!

PIRATES
So stealthily the pirate creeps,
While all the household soundly sleeps.
Come, friends, who plough the sea,
Truce to navigation;
Take another station;
Let's vary piracee
With a little burglaree!

POLICE (softly)
Tarantara, tarantara!

SAMUEL (distributing implements to various members of the gang)
Here's your crowbar and your centrebit,
Your life-preserver—you may want to hit!
Your silent matches, your dark lantern seize,
Take your file and your skeletonic keys.

POLICE
Tarantara!

PIRATES
With cat-like tread

POLICE
Tarantara!

PIRATES
in silence dread,

(Enter KING, FREDERIC and RUTH)

ALL (fortissimo).
With cat-like tread, etc.

RECITATIVE

FREDERIC
Hush, hush! not a word; I see a light inside!
The Major-Gen'ral comes, so quickly hide!

PIRATES
Yes, yes, the Major-General comes!

(Exeunt KING, FREDERIC, SAMUEL, and RUTH)

POLICE
Yes, yes, the Major-General comes!

GENERAL (entering in dressing-gown, carrying a light)
Yes, yes, the Major-General comes!

SOLO—**GENERAL**
Tormented with the anguish dread
Of falsehood unatoned,
I lay upon my sleepless bed,
And tossed and turned and groaned.
The man who finds his conscience ache
No peace at all enjoys;
And as I lay in bed awake,
I thought I heard a noise.

MEN
He thought he heard a noise—ha! ha!

GENERAL
No, all is still
In dale, on hill;
My mind is set at ease—
So still the scene,
It must have been
The sighing of the breeze.

BALLAD—**GENERAL**

Sighing softly to the river
Comes the loving breeze,
Setting nature all a-quiver,
Rustling through the trees.

MEN
Through the trees.

GENERAL
And the brook, in rippling measure,
Laughs for very love,
While the poplars, in their pleasure,
Wave their arms above.

MEN
Yes, the trees, for very love,
Wave their leafy arms above.

ALL
River, river, little river,
May thy loving prosper ever!
Heaven speed thee, poplar tree,
May thy wooing happy be.

GENERAL
Yet, the breeze is but a rover,
When he wings away,
Brook and poplar mourn a lover
Sighing, "Well-a-day!"

MEN
Well-a-day!

GENERAL
Ah! the doing and undoing,
That the rogue could tell!
When the breeze is out a-wooing,
Who can woo so well?

MEN
Shocking tales the rogue could tell,
Nobody can woo so well.

ALL
Pretty brook, thy dream is over,
For thy love is but a rover;
Sad the lot of poplar trees,
Courted by a fickle breeze!

(Enter the MAJOR-GENERAL's daughters, led by MABEL, all in white peignoirs and night-caps, and carrying lighted candles.)

GIRLS
Now what is this, and what is that, and why does father leave his rest
At such a time of night as this, so very incompletely dressed?
Dear father is, and always was, the most methodical of men!
It's his invariable rule to go to bed at half-past ten.
What strange occurrence can it be that calls dear father from his rest
At such a time of night as this, so very incompletely dressed?

(Enter KING, SAMUEL, and FREDERIC)

KING
Forward, my men, and seize that General there! His life is over.

(They seize the GENERAL)

GIRLS
The pirates! the pirates! Oh, despair!

PIRATES (springing up)
Yes, we're the pirates, so despair!

GENERAL
Frederic here! Oh, joy! Oh. rapture!
Summon your men and effect their capture!

MABEL
Frederic, save us!

FREDERIC
Beautiful Mabel,
I would if I could, but I am not able.

PIRATES
He's telling the truth, he is not able.

KING
With base deceit
You worked upon our feelings!
Revenge is sweet,
And flavours all our dealings!
With courage rare
And resolution manly,
For death prepare,
Unhappy Gen'ral Stanley.

MABEL (wildly)
Is he to die, unshriven, unannealed?

GIRLS
Oh, spare him!

MABEL
Will no one in his cause a weapon wield?

GIRLS
Oh, spare him!

POLICE (springing up)
Yes, we are here, though hitherto concealed!

GIRLS
Oh, rapture!

POLICE
So to Constabulary, pirates yield!

GIRLS
Oh, rapture!

(A struggle ensues between Pirates and Police, RUTH tackling the SERGEANT. Eventually the Police are overcome and fall prostrate, the Pirates standing over them with drawn swords.)

CHORUS OF PIRATES AND **POLICE**

PIRATES	POLICE
We triumph now, for well we trow	You triumph now, for well we trow
Your mortal career's cut short;	Our mortal career's cut short;
No pirate band will take its stand	No pirate band will take its stand
At the Central Criminal Court.	At the Central Criminal Court.

SERGEANT
To gain a brief advantage you've contrived,
But your proud triumph will not be long-lived

KING
Don't say you are orphans, for we know that game.

SERGEANT
On your allegiance we've a stronger claim.
We charge you yield, we charge you yield,
In Queen Victoria's name!

KING (baffled)
You do?

POLICE
We do!
We charge you yield,
In Queen Victoria's name!

(PIRATES kneel, POLICE stand over them triumphantly.)

KING
We yield at once, with humbled mien,
Because, with all our faults, we love our Queen.

POLICE
Yes, yes, with all their faults, they love their Queen.

ALL
Yes, yes, with all their faults, they love their Queen.

(POLICE, holding PIRATES by the collar, take out handkerchiefs and weep.)

GENERAL
Away with them, and place them at the bar!

(Enter RUTH)

RUTH
One moment! let me tell you who they are.
They are no members of the common throng;
They are all noblemen who have gone wrong.

ALL
They are all noblemen who have gone wrong.

GENERAL
No Englishman unmoved that statement hears,
Because, with all our faults, we love our House of Peers.

(ALL kneel)

I pray you, pardon me, ex-Pirate King!
Peers will be peers, and youth will have its fling.
Resume your ranks and legislative duties,
And take my daughters, all of whom are beauties.

FINALE—MABEL, EDITH and ENSEMBLE

Poor wandering ones!
Though ye have surely strayed,
Take heart of grace,
Your steps retrace,
Poor wandering ones!
Poor wandering ones!
If such poor love as ours
Can help you find
True peace of mind,
Why, take it, it is yours!

ALL
Poor wandering ones! etc.

CURTAIN

Sir William Schwenck Gilbert was born on November 18th, 1836 at 17 Southampton Street, Strand, London. His father, also named William, was a naval surgeon, who later became a writer of novels and short stories, some of which were illustrated by his son. Gilbert's mother was the former Anne Mary Bye Morris (1812–1888), the daughter of Thomas Morris, an apothecary.

Gilbert's parents were distant and stern, and there was no close bond between either themselves or their children (the marriage was to eventually break up in 1876). Gilbert had three younger sisters, Jane Morris, Anne Maude Mary Florence.

As a child, Gilbert was nicknamed "Bab".

The family travelled to Italy in 1838 and then France before finally returning to settle in London in 1847.

Gilbert was educated in Boulogne, France from age seven, then at Western Grammar School, Brompton, London, before the Great Ealing School, where he became head boy and wrote plays for school performances. He then attended King's College London, graduating in 1856.

His first thought for a career was to take examinations for a commission in the Royal Artillery, but the Crimean War had just ended and with fewer recruits needed only a commission in a line regiment was available. He opted instead for the Civil Service and was an assistant clerk in the Privy Council Office for four years. He hated it. In 1859 he joined the Militia, a part-time volunteer force, and served until 1878, as his other work allowed, and reached the rank of Captain.

To supplement his income Gilbert wrote a variety of stories, comic rants, theatre reviews (many in the form of a parody of the play being reviewed), and, using the pseudonym of his childhood nickname, "Bab" illustrated poems for several comic magazines, primarily Fun, started in 1861. His work was also published in the Cornhill Magazine, London Society, Tinsley's Magazine and Temple Bar. Gilbert was also the London correspondent for L'Invalide Russe and a drama critic for the Illustrated London Times. In the

1860s he also contributed to Tom Hood's Christmas annuals, to Saturday Night, the Comic News and the Savage Club Papers.

The poems, illustrated humorously by Gilbert, proved immensely popular and were reprinted in book form as the Bab Ballads. He would later return to many of these as source material for his plays and comic operas.

In 1863 he received a bequest of £300 allowing him to leave the civil service and attempt a career as a barrister. Unfortunately, he managed to attract few clients.

However, these events happily coincided with his first professionally produced play; Uncle Baby, which ran for seven weeks in the autumn of 1863.

In 1865–66, Gilbert collaborated with Charles Millward on several pantomimes, including Hush-a-Bye, Baby, On the Tree Top, or, Harlequin Fortunia, King Frog of Frog Island, and the Magic Toys of Lowther Arcade (1866).

Gilbert's first solo success, however, came a few days after Hush-a-Bye Baby premiered. His friend and mentor, Tom Robertson, was asked to deliver a pantomime within two weeks. Robertson couldn't and recommended Gilbert who took the job. Written and rushed to the stage in 10 days, Dulcamara, or the Little Duck and the Great Quack, a burlesque of Gaetano Donizetti's L'elisir d'amore, proved very popular. This led to a long series of further Gilbert opera burlesques, pantomimes and farces, full of dreadful puns, but showing signs of the satire that would later be such an integral part of Gilbert's work.

After a failed relationship with the novelist Annie Thomas, Gilbert married Lucy Agnes Turner, whom he affectionately called "Kitty", in 1867; she was 11 years his junior. They were socially active both in London and later at their new home at Grim's Dyke, often holding dinner parties. Although they had no children they had many pets, including several exotic ones.

Next followed Gilbert's biggest success so far; his penultimate operatic parody, Robert the Devil, a burlesque of Giacomo Meyerbeer's opera, Robert le diable, part of a triple bill that opened the Gaiety Theatre, London in 1868. It ran for over 100 nights.

In Victorian theatre, Gilbert's burlesques were considered very tasteful compared to the offerings of others. He would now move away from burlesque to plays with original plots and fewer puns. His first was An Old Score in 1869.

Theatre, at this time had fallen into disrepute. London was awash with poorly translated French operettas and cheaply written, prurient Victorian burlesques. From 1869 to 1875, Gilbert joined with Thomas German Reed (and his wife Priscilla), whose Gallery of Illustration sought to regain some of theatre's lost respect with family entertainments. This would be so successful that by 1885 Gilbert could safely state that original British plays were appropriate for an innocent 15-year-old girl to watch.

The initial work for the Gallery of Illustration, No Cards, was the first of six musical entertainments for the German Reeds, by Gilbert some with music composed by Thomas German Reed.

The German Reeds' intimate theatre allowed Gilbert to develop a personal style that would also cede to him control all aspects of production; set, costumes, direction and stage management.

Gilbert's first big hit at the Gallery of Illustration, Ages Ago, also opened in 1869. It marked the beginning of a collaboration with the composer Frederic Clay that would last seven years and cover four works. It was at a rehearsal for Ages Ago that Clay introduced Gilbert to Arthur Sullivan.

These musical works gave Gilbert a valuable education as a lyricist and he perfected the 'topsy-turvy' style that he had been developing in his Bab Ballads, where the humour was derived by setting up a ridiculous premise and following through on its logical consequences, however absurd they might be.

Ever busy he found time to create several 'fairy comedies' at the Haymarket Theatre. The premise was the idea of self-revelation by characters under the influence of magic or some supernatural experience. The first was The Palace of Truth (1870), based partly on a story by Madame de Genlis. In 1871, with Pygmalion and Galatea, one of seven plays that he produced that year, Gilbert scored his greatest hit to date. Together, these plays including The Wicked World (1873), Sweethearts (1874), and Broken Hearts (1875), did for Gilbert on the dramatic stage what the German Reed entertainments had done for him on the musical stage: they established that his talents were large and burgeoning, a writer of wide range, as comfortable with human drama as much as farcical humour.

Contemptorous with this period Gilbert pushed the satirical boundaries. He collaborated with Gilbert Arthur à Beckett on The Happy Land (1873), in part, a parody of his own The Wicked World, which was briefly banned because of its caricatures of Gladstone and his ministers. Similarly, The Realm of Joy (1873) was set in the lobby of a theatre performing a scandalous play (implied to be the Happy Land), with many jokes at the expense of the Lord Chamberlain (the "Lord High Disinfectant", as he's referred to in the play). In Charity (1874), however, Gilbert uses the freedom of the stage in a different way: to illuminate the contrasting ways in which society treated men and women who had sex outside of marriage. It was ground breaking and some see it as anticipating the 'problem plays' of Shaw and Ibsen.

Once established as a writer Gilbert was also the stage director, with strong, forceful opinions on how they should best be performed.

In Gilbert's 1874 burlesque, Rosencrantz and Guildenstern, the character Hamlet, in his speech to the players, sums up Gilbert's theory of comic acting: "I hold that there is no such antick fellow as your bombastical hero who doth so earnestly spout forth his folly as to make his hearers believe that he is unconscious of all incongruity". Again some say with this he prepared the ground for playwrights such as George Bernard Shaw and Oscar Wilde to be able to flourish.

Tom Robertson had "introduced Gilbert both to the revolutionary notion of disciplined rehearsals and to mise-en-scène or unity of style in the whole presentation – direction, design, music, acting." Like Robertson, Gilbert demanded discipline in his actors, that they know their lines, enunciate them clearly and keep to his stage directions, a new development for actors at the time. It also ushered in the replacement of the star with the disciplined ensemble.

Gilbert was meticulous in his preparations, making models of the stage and designing every action in advance. He refused to work with actors who challenged him. He was famous for demonstrating the action himself, even as he grew older. Such was his interest in standards that even during long runs and revivals, he closely supervised the performances of his plays, making sure that no one made additions or deletions.

Arthur Sullivan – A Short Biography

Sir Arthur Seymour Sullivan, MVO was born on May 13th 1842 in Lambeth, London. His father, Thomas Sullivan, a military bandmaster, clarinetist and music teacher, was born in Ireland and raised in Chelsea, London, and his mother, Mary Clementina (née Coghlan, English born, of Irish and Italian descent. Thomas Sullivan was based from 1845 to 1857 at the Royal Military College, Sandhurst, where he was the bandmaster and taught music privately to supplement his income. Young Sullivan became proficient with many of the instruments in the band and had composed an anthem, "By the waters of Babylon", by the age of eight. While proudly observing his son's obvious musical talent, he knew, at first hand, how insecure a profession it was and discouraged him from pursuing it.

Three years later whilst at a private school in Bayswater, Sullivan persuaded his parents and headmaster to allow him to apply for membership in the choir of the Chapel Royal. There were concerns that Sullivan at nearly 12 years of age was too old to be a treble as his voice would soon break. But he was accepted and soon became a soloist and, by 1856, was promoted to "first boy". Troublingly, even at this age, Sullivan's health was delicate, and he was easily fatigued.

However, Sullivan flourished under the training of the Reverend Thomas Helmore, and began to compose anthems and songs. Helmore arranged for one pieces, "O Israel", to be published in 1855.

In 1856, the Royal Academy of Music awarded the first Mendelssohn Scholarship to the 14-year-old Sullivan, granting him a year's training at the academy. His principal teacher there was John Goss, whose own teacher had been a pupil of Mozart. Initially Sullivan studied piano.

Sullivan's scholarship was extended to a second year, and then a third so that he could study in Germany, at the Leipzig Conservatoire. There he was trained in Mendelssohn's ideas and techniques as well as being exposed to Schubert, Verdi, Bach, and Wagner. Sullivan was an eager pupil and always looking for inspiration. On a visit to a synagogue, he was so struck by some of the cadences and progressions in the music that three decades later he would recall them for use in his serious opera, Ivanhoe.

Though the scholarship in Leipzig, was for one year he stayed for three. Sullivan credited his Leipzig period with rapid and sustained musical growth. His graduation piece, in 1861, was a set of incidental music to Shakespeare's The Tempest. Revised and expanded, it was performed at the Crystal Palace in 1862, a year after his return to London. It was an immediate sensation. He began building a reputation as England's most promising young composer.

He now embarked on composing with a series of ambitious works, interspersed with hymns, parlour songs and other light pieces of a more commercial nature. These compositions could not support him financially, and from 1861 to 1872 he supplemented his income working as a church organist, a task he enjoyed, and as a music teacher, sometimes at the Crystal Palace School, which he hated and gave up as soon as his finances allowed. Sullivan also took an early chance to compose pieces for royalty with the wedding of the Prince of Wales in 1863.

Sullivan began to put voice and orchestra together with The Masque at Kenilworth (Birmingham Festival, 1864). For Covent Garden that same year he composed his first ballet, L'Île Enchantée.

1865 saw Sullivan initiated into Freemasonry and was Grand Organist of the United Grand Lodge of England in 1887 during Queen Victoria's Golden Jubilee.

In 1866, he premiered his Irish Symphony and Cello Concerto, his only works in these genres. In the same year, his Overture in C (In Memoriam), commemorating the recent death of his father, was a commission from the Norwich Festival.

His overture Marmion was premiered by the Philharmonic Society in 1867. The Times called it "another step in advance on the part of the only composer of any remarkable promise that just at present we can boast."

Sadly, his initial attempt at opera, The Sapphire Necklace (1863–64) with a libretto by Henry F. Chorley, was not produced and, apart from the Overture and two songs published separately, is now lost.

His first surviving opera, Cox and Box (1866), was written for a private performance. It then received charity performances in London and Manchester, and was later produced at the Gallery of Illustration, where it ran for an extraordinary 264 performances. His soon to be partner, W. S. Gilbert, writing in Fun magazine, announced the score as superior to F. C. Burnand's libretto.

In 1867 Sullivan and Burnand were commissioned by Thomas German Reed for a two-act opera, The Contrabandista (revised and expanded as The Chieftain in 1894), but it was a much more modest success.

Sullivan wrote a group of seven part songs in 1868, the best-known of which is "The Long Day Closes". His last major work of the 1860s was a short oratorio, The Prodigal Son, which premiered in Worcester Cathedral as part of the 1869 Three Choirs Festival to much praise.

The Overture di Ballo, Sullivan's most enduring work, was composed for the Birmingham Festival in 1870.

1871 was a busy year. Sullivan published his only song cycle, The Window; or, The Songs of the Wrens, to words by Tennyson, and wrote the first of a series of suites of incidental music for West End productions of Shakespeare plays. Later in the year he composed a dramatic cantata, On Shore and Sea, for the opening of the London International Exhibition, and the beautiful hymn Onward, Christian Soldiers, with words by Sabine Baring-Gould. The Salvation Army adopted it and it has become one of Britain's best loved hymns.

Gilbert & Sullivan – The Collaboration Begins

In 1871, John Hollingshead commissioned Gilbert to work with Sullivan on a holiday piece for Christmas, entitled Thespis, or The Gods Grown Old, at the Gaiety Theatre. It was a success and its run was extended beyond the length of the Gaiety's normal run. And that seemed to be that.

Gilbert and Sullivan now went their separate ways. Gilbert worked again with Clay on Happy Arcadia (1872), and with Alfred Cellier on Topsyturveydom (1874), as well as several farces, operetta libretti, extravaganzas, fairy comedies, adaptations from novels, translations from the French. In 1874, he published his last piece for Fun magazine ("Rosencrantz and Guildenstern"), almost three years after his last and then promptly resigned citing disapproval of the new owner's other publishing interests.

Sullivan was busy on large-scale works in the early 1870s with the Festival Te Deum (Crystal Palace, 1872); and the oratorio, The Light of the World (Birmingham Festival, 1873). He also wrote suites of incidental music for productions of The Merry Wives of Windsor at the Gaiety in 1874 and Henry VIII at the Theatre Royal, Manchester in 1877 as well as continuing composing hymns.

In 1873, Sullivan had also contributed songs to Burnand's Christmas "drawing room extravaganza", The Miller and His Man.

By 1875 conditions were right for Gilbert and Sullivan to work together again. Back in 1868, Gilbert had published a short comedic libretto in Fun magazine entitled "Trial by Jury: An Operetta". In 1873, Gilbert had arranged with theatrical manager and composer, Carl Rosa, to expand this work into a one-act libretto. It was arranged that Rosa's wife was to sing the role of the plaintiff. Tragically, Rosa's wife died in childbirth in 1874. Gilbert offered the libretto to Richard D'Oyly Carte, but Carte could not use the piece at that time.

The project seemed grounded. A few months later Carte, was managing the Royalty Theatre, needed a short piece to pair with Offenbach's La Périchole. Carte had previously conducted Sullivan's Cox and Box and remembering that Gilbert had suggested a libretto to him, he reunited Gilbert and Sullivan. The result was the one-act comic opera Trial by Jury. Starring Sullivan's brother Fred as the Learned Judge, it became a surprise hit, as well as earning lavish praise from the critics. It played for over 300 performances in its first few seasons.

A short time after Trial had opened Sullivan wrote The Zoo, another one-act comic opera, with a libretto by B. C. Stephenson. It did not perform well. Now the path was clear for Gilbert & Sullivan to reteam together in earnest and dominate light opera for the next 15 years.

Light opera was not considered of much worth by serious critics. Gilbert wanted greater respect for himself and his profession. At that time plays were not published in a form suitable for a "gentleman's library", they were in the main cheap and unattractive in their look designed mainly for use by actors rather than the home reader. Gilbert now arranged in late 1875 for the publishers Chatto and Windus to print a volume of his plays in a format designed to appeal to the general reader, with an attractive binding and clear type, containing Gilbert's most respectable plays, including his most serious works, and mischievously capped off with Trial by Jury.

After the success of Trial by Jury, there were discussions towards reviving Thespis, but Gilbert and Sullivan were not able to agree on terms with Carte and his backers. The score to Thespis was never published, and tragically most of the music is now lost.

Carte took some time to gather together funds for another opera, and in this gap the ever-busy Gilbert produced several works including Tom Cobb (1875), Eyes and No Eyes (1875), and Princess Toto (1876), his last and most ambitious work with Clay, a three-act comic opera with full orchestra. He also found time to write two serious works, Broken Hearts (1875) and Dan'l Druce, Blacksmith (1876) and his most successful comic play, Engaged (1877), which inspired Oscar Wilde's The Importance of Being Earnest.

It was only by 1877 that Carte finally assembled enough investors to form the Comedy Opera Company with a mandate to launch a series of original English comic operas, beginning with a third collaboration between Gilbert and Sullivan, The Sorcerer, in November 1877.

The Sorcerer (1877), ran for 178 performances, a success by the standards of the day, but H.M.S. Pinafore (1878), which followed it, turned Gilbert and Sullivan into an international phenomenon. The bright and cheerful music of Pinafore was composed during a time when Sullivan was in the middle of a health scare. He was in terrible pain from a kidney stone. H.M.S. Pinafore ran for 571 performances in London, the then-second-longest theatrical run in history, it also gave birth to and more than 150 unauthorised productions in America alone. Although this increased the reach of their reputations it added nothing to their profits.

It was noted in the Times review of H.M.S. Pinafore that the opera was an early attempt at the establishment of a "national musical stage" ... free from risqué French "improprieties" and without the "aid" of Italian and German musical models.

As the profits rolled in came acrimony among the investors who felt the shares were unequal. One night the other Comedy Opera Company partners hired thugs to storm the theatre to steal the sets and costumes in order that they could mount a rival production. This was beaten off by stagehands and others at the theatre loyal to Carte. Carte was to now continue as sole impresario of the newly renamed D'Oyly Carte Opera Company.

For the next decade, the Savoy Operas were Gilbert's principal activity. The successful comic operas with Sullivan continued to appear every year or two, several of them being among the longest-running productions of the musical stage. After Pinafore came The Pirates of Penzance (1879), Patience (1881), Iolanthe (1882), Princess Ida (1884 and based on Gilbert's earlier farce, The Princess), The Mikado (1885), Ruddigore (1887), The Yeomen of the Guard (1888), and The Gondoliers (1889). Gilbert not only directed and oversaw all aspects of production, but he designed the costumes himself for Patience, Iolanthe, Princess Ida, and Ruddigore. He insisted on precise and authentic sets and costumes, which provided a foundation to ground and focus his absurd characters and situations.

In 1878, Gilbert realised a lifelong dream to play Harlequin, which he did at the Gaiety Theatre in an amateur charity production of The Forty Thieves, written partly by himself. Gilbert trained for Harlequin's stylised dancing with his friend John D'Auban, who had arranged the dances for some of his plays and would choreograph most of the Gilbert and Sullivan operas. Producer John Hollingshead later remembered, "the gem of the performance was the grimly earnest and determined Harlequin of W. S. Gilbert. It gave me an idea of what Oliver Cromwell would have made of the character."

In 1879, Sullivan suggested to a reporter from The New York Times the secret of his success with Gilbert: "His ideas are as suggestive for music as they are quaint and laughable. His numbers ... always give me musical ideas."

During this time, Gilbert and Sullivan also collaborated on one other major work. In 1880, Sullivan was appointed director of the triennial Leeds Music Festival. For his first festival he was commissioned to write a sacred choral work. He chose Henry Hart Milman's 1822 dramatic poem based on the life and death of Saint Margaret the Virgin for its basis. It premiered at the Leeds music festival in October 1880. Gilbert arranged the original epic poem by Henry Hart Milman into a libretto suitable for the music.

Carte opened the next Gilbert and Sullivan piece, Patience, in April 1881 at London's Opera Comique, where their past three operas had played. In October, Patience transferred to the new, larger, state-of-the-art (it was the first theatre to be lit entirely with electricity) Savoy Theatre, built with the profits of the previous Gilbert and Sullivan works.

From now on all of the partnership's collaborations were produced at the Savoy. The first to actually premiere here was Iolanthe in 1882, it was their fourth hit in a row.

Cracks were beginning to surface between the partners. Sullivan, despite the financial security, began to view his work with Gilbert as beneath his skills, as well as being repetitious. After Iolanthe, Sullivan had not intended to write a new work with Gilbert, but when his broker went bankrupt in late 1882 he suffered serious financial loss. Needs must and Sullivan buckled down to continue writing Savoy operas. In February 1883, he and Gilbert signed a five-year agreement with Carte, requiring them to produce a new comic opera on six months' notice.

The ever watchful Gilbert had the previous year installed a telephone in his home and another at the prompt desk at the Savoy Theatre, so that he could listen in on performances and rehearsals from his home study. Gilbert had referred to the new technology in Pinafore in 1878, only two years after the device was invented and before London even had telephones.

Better news arrived for Sullivan on May 22nd, 1883, when he was knighted by Queen Victoria for his "services ... rendered to the promotion of the art of music" in Britain. The musical establishment, and many critics, believed that this would put an end to his career as a composer of comic opera – that a musical knight should not stoop below oratorio or grand opera. But Sullivan having just signed the five-year agreement and the financial security that gave him could no nothing to change course now.

The next opera, Princess Ida in 1884, which was the duo's only three-act, blank verse work, stuttered. Its run was much shorter. Sullivan's score was praised but with box office receipts lagging in March 1884, Carte gave the six months' notice, under the partnership contract, requiring a new opera.

Sullivan's friend, composer Frederic Clay, had suffered a serious stroke in early December 1883 that ended his career at only 45 years of age. Sullivan, with his own longstanding kidney problems, and his desire to devote himself to more serious music, replied to Carte, "It is impossible for me to do another piece of the character of those already written by Gilbert and myself."

Gilbert however was already at work on it. His idea revolved around a plot in which people fell in love against their wills after taking a magic lozenge. Sullivan was unequoviacal in his response. On April 1st, 1884 he wrote that he had "come to the end of my tether with the operas. I have been continually keeping down the music in order that not one syllable should be lost.... I should like to set a story of human interest & probability where the humorous words would come in a humorous not serious situation, & where, if the situation were a tender or dramatic one the words would be of similar character."

There was now a lengthy exchange of correspondence in which Sullivan called Gilbert's plot sketch (particularly the "lozenge" element) unacceptably mechanical, and too similar in both its grotesque "elements of topsyturveydom" and in actual plot to their earlier work, especially The Sorcerer, and requested, time and again, that a new subject be found.

This impasse was finally resolved on May 8th when Gilbert proposed a plot that would be their most successful: The Mikado (1885). It was to run for a staggering 672 performances.

In 1886, Sullivan composed his last large-scale choral work of the decade. It was a cantata for the Leeds Festival, The Golden Legend, based on Longfellow's poem of the same name. Apart from the comic operas, this proved to be Sullivan's best received full-length work. It was given hundreds of performances during his lifetime alone.

Ruddigore followed The Mikado in 1887. It was profitable, but its nine-month run was deemed to be disappointing compared with the earlier Savoy operas.

Gilbert was always keen to use a good idea again and proposed for their next piece another version of the magic lozenge plot. It was immediately rejected by Sullivan. Gilbert finally proposed a quite serious opera, to which Sullivan was in agreement. Although not a grand opera, The Yeomen of the Guard (1888) gave him the opportunity to compose his most ambitious stage work to date. In 1885, Sullivan had told an interviewer, ""The opera of the future is a compromise (among the French, German and Italian schools) – a sort of eclectic school, a selection of the merits of each one. I myself will make an attempt to produce a grand opera of this new school. ... Yes, it will be an historical work, and it is the dream of my life."

After The Yeomen of the Guard opened, Sullivan turned once again to Shakespeare and composed incidental music for Henry Irving's production of Macbeth (1888).

Sullivan wished to produce further serious works with Gilbert. He had collaborated with no other librettist since 1875. Gilbert felt the reaction to The Yeomen of the Guard had "not been so convincing as to warrant us in assuming that the public want something more earnest still." Gilbert countered by proposing that Sullivan should go ahead with his plan to write a grand opera, as well as comic works for the Savoy. Sullivan was not immediately persuaded. He replied, "I have lost the liking for writing comic opera, and entertain very grave doubts as to my power of doing it."

Nevertheless, Sullivan soon commissioned a grand opera libretto from Julian Sturgis (the recommendation came from Gilbert), while suggesting to Gilbert that he revive an old idea for an opera set in colourful Venice. The comic opera was completed first in 1889. The Gondoliers has been described as a pinnacle of Sullivan's achievement. It was to be the last great Gilbert and Sullivan success.

In April 1890, during the run of The Gondoliers, Gilbert objected to Carte's financial accounts which included a charge to the partnership for the cost of new carpeting for the Savoy Theatre lobby. Gilbert believed that this was a maintenance expense that should be charged to Carte alone. Carte who was building a new theatre to present Sullivan's forthcoming grand opera was adamant that it was legitimate. Sullivan sided with Carte, even going so far as to testify erroneously as to certain old debts.

The partners were in fundamental disagreement and the relationship was for all intents and purposes ruptured.

Gilbert took legal action against Carte and Sullivan and refused to write a word more for the Savoy. Sullivan wrote to Gilbert in September 1890 that he was "physically and mentally ill over this wretched business. I have not yet got over the shock of seeing our names coupled ... in hostile antagonism over a few miserable pounds".

From Gilbert's point of view Carte had either made a series of serious blunders in the accounts, or deliberately attempted to swindle his partners.

Gilbert wrote to Sullivan on May 28th, 1891, a year after the end of the "Quarrel", that Carte had admitted "an unintentional overcharge of nearly £1,000 in the electric lighting accounts alone." It seemed to illustrate Gilbert's point.

Work beckoned for Gilbert and he got on with it. He wrote The Mountebanks with Alfred Cellier and then a flop Haste to the Wedding with George Grossmith. Sullivan wrote Haddon Hall with Sydney Grundy.

In the Courts Gilbert prevailed in the lawsuit and felt vindicated. Although there was acrimony and bitterness between them the partnership had been so profitable that, after the financial failure of the Royal English Opera House, Carte and his wife sought to reunite the author and composer.

In 1891, after numerous failed attempts at a reconciliation, Tom Chappell, the music publisher who printed the Gilbert and Sullivan operas, stepped in to mediate between his two most profitable artists, and within two weeks, against the odds, had succeeded. The result was to be two more operas: Utopia, Limited (1893) and The Grand Duke (1896).

A third was almost achieved when Gilbert offered a third libretto to Sullivan (His Excellency, 1894), but his insistence on casting Nancy McIntosh, his protegée from Utopia, led to Sullivan's refusal.

Utopia, was only a modest success, and The Grand Duke, in which a theatrical troupe, by means of a "statutory duel" and a conspiracy, takes political control of a grand duchy, was a failure.

The partnership now ended for good.

Graciously Gilbert would late write, "... Savoy opera was snuffed out by the deplorable death of my distinguished collaborator, Sir Arthur Sullivan. When that event occurred, I saw no one with whom I felt that I could work with satisfaction and success, and so I discontinued to write libretti."

WS Gilbert – Life After the Partnership

In 1889 Gilbert financed the building of the Garrick Theatre. The following year the Gilberts moved to Grim's Dyke in Harrow. In 1891, Gilbert was appointed Justice of the Peace for Middlesex. After casting Nancy McIntosh in Utopia, Limited, he and Lady Gilbert developed an affection for her, and she eventually gained the status of an unofficially adopted daughter, moving to Grim's Dyke to live with them. She continued living there, even after Gilbert's death, until Lady Gilbert's death in 1936.

Although Gilbert announced a retirement from the theatre after the poor initial run of his last work with Sullivan, The Grand Duke (1896) and the poor reception of his 1897 play The Fortune Hunter, he produced at least three more plays over the last dozen years of his life, including an unsuccessful opera, Fallen Fairies (1909), with Edward German.

Gilbert, as we know was very keen on keeping his plays in the shape they were originally intended and continued to supervise the various revivals of his works by the D'Oyly Carte Opera Company, including its London Repertory seasons in 1906–09.

The last play he wrote, The Hooligan, produced just four months before his death, is a study of a young condemned thug in a prison cell. Gilbert shows sympathy for his protagonist, the son of a thief who, brought up among thieves, kills his girlfriend.

This grim, yet powerful piece, became one of Gilbert's most successful serious dramas, and it is easy to see why many thought he was developing a new style only for death to rob of us of what would surely be a fascinating journey.

In these last years, Gilbert wrote children's book versions of H.M.S. Pinafore and The Mikado giving, in some cases, backstory that is not found in the librettos.

Official recognition for him came on July 15th, 1907 with his knighthood in recognition of his contributions to drama. Gilbert was the first British writer ever to receive a knighthood for his plays alone—earlier dramatist knights were knighted for political and other services.

On May 29th, 1911, Gilbert was about to give a swimming lesson to Winifred Isabel Emery and 17-year-old Ruby Preece in the lake of his home, Grim's Dyke, when Preece lost her footing and called for help. Gilbert dived in to save her but suffered a heart attack in the middle of the lake and died.

William Schwenck was cremated at Golders Green and his ashes buried at the Church of St. John the Evangelist, Stanmore. The inscription on Gilbert's memorial on the south wall of the Thames Embankment in London reads: "His Foe was Folly, and his Weapon Wit".

George Grossmith wrote to The Daily Telegraph that, although Gilbert had been described as an autocrat at rehearsals, "That was really only his manner when he was playing the part of stage director at rehearsals. As a matter of fact, he was a generous, kind true gentleman, and I use the word in the purest and original sense."

Gilbert's legacy, aside from building the Garrick Theatre are the canon of Savoy Operas and other works that are either still being performed or in print all these years later. He has made a lasting and defining influence on both the American and British musical theatre. The innovations in content and form of the works that he and Sullivan developed, and in Gilbert's theories of acting and stage direction, directly influenced the development of the modern musical throughout the 20th century. Gilbert's lyrics use punning, as well as complex internal and two and three-syllable rhyme schemes, and served as a model for such 20th century Broadway lyricists as P.G. Wodehouse, Cole Porter, Ira Gershwin, and Lorenz Hart.

Gilbert's influence on the English language has also been marked, with well-known phrases such as "A policeman's lot is not a happy one", "short, sharp shock", "What never? Well, hardly ever!", and "let the punishment fit the crime" arising from his pen.

Sullivan's only grand opera, Ivanhoe, based on Walter Scott's novel, opened at Carte's new Royal English Opera House on January 31st, 1891. Sullivan completed the score too late to meet Carte's planned production date, and costs had overrun to such an extent that Carte insisted on a contractual penalty of £3,000 for the delay. However, when it opened it ran 155 consecutive performances, a wonderful run for a serious opera, and garnered good reviews. Afterwards, Carte was unable to fill the new opera house with other productions, and, unfairly, Ivanhoe was blamed for the failure of the opera house.

Later in 1891, New York beckoned for Sullivan and his music for Tennyson's The Foresters, which ran at Daly's Theatre in New York in 1892, but failed in London the following year.

Sullivan returned to comic opera, but needed a new collaborator. His next piece was Haddon Hall in 1892, with a libretto by Sydney Grundy based somewhat loosely on the elopement of Dorothy Vernon with John Manners. Although still comic, the tone and style of the work was more serious and romantic than the operas with Gilbert. It nonetheless enjoyed a run of 204 performances, and earned critical praise.

In 1894 Sullivan teamed up again with F. C. Burnand for The Chieftain, a heavily-reworked version of their earlier two-act opera, The Contrabandista, alas it failed.

The following year Sullivan provided incidental music for the Lyceum, this time for J. Comyns Carr's King Arthur.

As we know Gilbert and Sullivan did reunite for The Grand Duke in 1896. But it failed and they never worked together again. This did not affect the constant revival of their earlier operas at the Savoy.

In May 1897, Sullivan's full-length ballet, Victoria and Merrie England, opened at the Alhambra Theatre in celebration of the Queen's Diamond Jubilee. The work's seven scenes celebrate English history and culture, with the Victorian period as the grand finale. It ran for six months which was a great achievement. Following this was The Beauty Stone in 1898, with a libretto by Arthur Wing Pinero and J. Comyns Carr. Based on mediaeval morality plays the opera was a critical failure and, on the whole, a commercial failure running for only seven weeks.

Success came in 1899, to benefit "the wives and children of soldiers and sailors" on active service in the Boer War, when Sullivan composed the music of a jingoistic song, "The Absent-Minded Beggar", to a text by Rudyard Kipling. It was a sensation and raised a staggering £250,000 from performances and the sale of sheet music and other merchandise. Later that year he returned to his comic roots with In The Rose of Persia, with a libretto by Basil Hood overlapping a setting of exotic Arabian Nights with plot elements of The Mikado. It was well received, and, apart from those with Gilbert, was his most successful full-length collaboration. Another opera with Hood, The Emerald Isle, quickly went into preparation, but sadly Sullivan died before it completion.

On November 22nd, 1900 Arthur Seymour Sullivan died of heart failure, following an attack of bronchitis, at his flat in London. The unfinished opera, The Emerald Isle, was completed by Edward German and premiered in 1901. His Te Deum Laudamus, written to commemorate the end of the Boer War, was performed posthumously.

Sullivan wished to be buried in Brompton Cemetery with his parents and brother, but by order of the Queen he was buried in St. Paul's Cathedral. In addition to his knighthood, honours awarded to Sullivan in his lifetime included Doctor in Music, honoris causa, by the universities of Cambridge (1876) and Oxford (1879); Chevalier, Légion d'honneur, France (1878); The Order of the Medjidieh conferred by the Sultan of Turkey (1888); and appointment as a Member of the Fourth Class of the Royal Victorian Order (MVO) in 1897.

In all, Sullivan's artistic output included 23 operas, 13 major orchestral works, eight choral works and oratorios, two ballets, one song cycle, incidental music to several plays, numerous hymns and other church pieces, and a large body of songs, parlour ballads, part songs, carols, and piano and chamber pieces.

Although Sullivan had several long term affairs and was also known to have a roving eye that led him to frequent liaisons with many other women he never married.

Rachel Scott Russell was the first of his great loves. Her parents' disapproval meant they met secretly but by 1868, Sullivan was enmeshed in a simultaneous and secret affair with Rachel's sister Louise. Both relationships had ceased by early 1869.

Sullivan's affair with the American socialite, Fanny Ronalds, a woman three years his senior, who had two children began when they met in Paris around 1867. The affair began in earnest soon after she moved to London in 1871. Despite his wandering ways she was a constant companion up to the time of Sullivan's death, but around 1889 or 1890, the sexual relationship seems to have ended.

In 1896, the 54-year-old Sullivan proposed marriage to 22-year-old Violet Beddington but she refused.

The favourite playgrounds for Sullivan were Paris and the south of France, with friends ranging from European royalty to Claude Debussy, and where the casinos enabled him to indulge his passion for gambling.

Sullivan enjoyed playing tennis although, according to George Grossmith, "I have seen some bad lawn-tennis players in my time, but I never saw anyone so bad as Arthur Sullivan".

He was devoted to his parents, particularly his mother, until her death in 1882. Henry Lytton wrote, "I believe there was never a more affectionate tie than that which existed between Sullivan and his mother, a very witty old lady, and one who took an exceptional pride in her son's accomplishments.

Sullivan once explained his method of working; "I don't use the piano in composition – that would limit me terribly". Sullivan explained that he did not wait for inspiration, but had "to dig for it. ... I decide on the rhythm before I come to the question of melody. ... I mark out the metre in dots and dashes, and not until I have quite settled on the rhythm do I proceed to actual notation."

In composing the Savoy operas, Sullivan wrote the vocal lines of the musical numbers first, and these were given to the actors. He, or an assistant, improvised a piano accompaniment at the early rehearsals; he wrote the orchestrations later, after he had seen what Gilbert's stage business would be. He left the overtures until last and often delegated their composition, based on his outlines, to his assistants, often adding his suggestions or corrections. Those Sullivan wrote himself include Thespis, Iolanthe, Princess Ida, The Yeomen of the Guard, The Gondoliers, The Grand Duke and probably Utopia Limited. Most of the overtures are structured as a potpourri of tunes from the operas in three sections: fast, slow and fast. The overtures from the Gilbert and Sullivan operas remain popular. Sullivan invariably conducted the operas on their opening nights.

In general, Sullivan preferred to write in major keys. In the Savoy operas less than 5% of the numbers are in a minor key and even in his serious works the major prevails. Sullivan was happy on occasion to use chords traditionally considered technically incorrect. When reproached for using consecutive fifths in Cox and Box, he replied "if 5ths turn up it doesn't matter, so long as there is no offence to the ear."

Sullivan's orchestra for the Savoy Operas was typical of any other pit orchestra of his era: 2 flutes (+ piccolo), oboe, 2 clarinets, bassoon, 2 horns, 2 cornets, 2 trombones, timpani, percussion and strings. According to Geoffrey Toye, the number of players in the Savoy orchestra was originally 31. Sullivan argued hard for an increase in the pit orchestra's size, and starting with The Yeomen of the Guard, the orchestra was augmented with a second bassoon and a bass trombone. Sullivan generally orchestrated each score at almost the last moment, noting that the accompaniment for an opera had to wait until he saw the staging, so that he could judge how heavily or lightly to orchestrate each part of the music. For his large-scale orchestral pieces, Sullivan added a second oboe part, sometimes double bassoon and bass clarinet, more horns, trumpets, tuba, and sometimes an organ and/or a harp. Many of these pieces used very large orchestras.

Sullivan's critical reputation has undergone extreme changes since he first came to prominence in the 1860s. At first, critics were struck by his potential, and he was hailed as the long-awaited great English composer. His incidental music to The Tempest received an acclaimed premiere at the Crystal Palace just before Sullivan's 20th birthday in April 1862. The Athenaeum wrote:

When Sullivan turned to comic opera with Gilbert, the serious critics began to express disapproval. Peter Gammond writes of "misapprehensions and prejudices, delivered to our door by the Victorian firm Musical Snobs Ltd. ... frivolity and high spirits were sincerely seen as elements that could not be exhibited by anyone who was to be admitted to the sanctified society of Art." As early as 1877 The Figaro wrote that Sullivan "has all the ability to make him a great composer, but he wilfully throws his opportunity away. ... He possesses all the natural ability to have given us an English opera, and, instead, he affords us a little more-or-less excellent fooling." Few critics denied the excellence of Sullivan's theatre scores. The Theatre wrote that "Iolanthe sustains Dr Sullivan's reputation as the most spontaneous, fertile, and scholarly composer of comic opera this country has ever produced." However, comic opera, no matter how skilfully crafted, was viewed as an intrinsically lower form of art than oratorio. The Athenaeum's review of The Martyr of Antioch declared: "It is an advantage to have the composer of H.M.S. Pinafore occupying himself with a worthier form of art."

Although the more solemn members of the musical establishment could not forgive Sullivan for writing music that was both comic and accessible, he was, nevertheless, "the nation's de facto composer laureate".

Gilbert & Sullivan – A Concise Bibliography

The Collaborative Pieces

All of these operas are full-length two-act works, except for Trial by Jury, which is in one act, and Princess Ida, which is three acts.

Thespis (1871)
Trial by Jury (1875)
The Sorcerer (1877)
H.M.S. Pinafore (1878)
The Pirates of Penzance (1879)
Patience (1881)
Iolanthe (1882)
Princess Ida (1884)
The Mikado (1885)
Ruddigore (1887)
The Yeomen of the Guard (1888)
The Gondoliers (1889)
Utopia, Limited (1893)
The Grand Duke (1896)

W.S. Gilbert – his Other Works

Poetry
The Bab Ballads, a collection of comic verse published roughly between 1865 and 1871
Songs of a Savoyard, London, 1890, a collection of Gilbert's song lyrics.

Short Stories
Foggerty's Fairy & Other Tales, a collection of short stories and essays, mainly from before 1874.

Some other short stories but not in the above appear here:-

Belgravia, Vol. 2 (1867). "From St. Paul's to Piccadilly," pp. 67–74
Fun, Vol. 1 new series (1865-1866) (several contributions by Gilbert; near end of volume)
Fun Christmas Number 1865, ("The Astounding Adventure of Wheeler J. Calamity,")
London Society, Vol. 13 (1868) (three "Thumbnail Sketches" by Gilbert)
On the Cards: Routledge's Christmas Annual (1867) ("Diamonds," and "The Converted Clown,")

Other Books
The Pinafore Picture Book, 1908, retelling the story of H.M.S. Pinafore for children, in prose narrative
The Story of The Mikado, 1921, a similar retelling of The Mikado for children

Plays and Musical Stage Works
Selected stage works that were important to Gilbert's career or were otherwise notable, in chronological order, excluding those listed under other headings below:

Dulcamara, or the Little Duck and the Great Quack (1866)

La Vivandière (1867)

Harlequin Cock Robin and Jenny Wren (1867), a Christmas pantomime.

The Merry Zingara (1868)

Robert the Devil (1868), it opened the Gaiety Theatre, London and ran in the provinces for 3 years.

The Pretty Druidess (1869), a parody of Norma – the last of Gilbert's five "operatic burlesques"

An Old Score (1869) (rewritten as "Quits!" in 1872) Gilbert's first full-length comedy.

The Princess (1870). Musical farce; the precursor to Princess Ida.

The Palace of Truth (1870).

Creatures of Impulse (1871), music by Alberto Randegger. From Gilberts story "A Strange Old Lady".

Pygmalion and Galatea (1871).

Randall's Thumb (1871). A comedy that opened the Royal Court Theatre.

The Wicked World (1873).

The Happy Land (1873). This work was briefly banned for its sharp satire of government ministers.

The Realm of Joy (1873).

The Wedding March (1873) a farce adapted from Un Chapeau de Paille d'Italie.

Rosencrantz & Guildenstern (published 1874, performed 1891). Gilbert's burlesque of Hamlet.

Charity (1874). Concerns Victorian attitudes towards sex outside of marriage.

Sweethearts (1874).

Tom Cobb (1875).

Broken Hearts (1875). The last of Gilbert's "fairy comedies", this was one of Gilbert's favourite plays.

Dan'l Druce, Blacksmith (1876).

Engaged (1877).

The Ne'er-do-Weel (1878); rewritten as "The Vagabond" after a few weeks.

The Forty Thieves (1878). Co-written with three other writers, WSG played Harlequin.

Gretchen (1879)

Foggerty's Fairy (1881)

Brantinghame Hall (1888) Gilbert's biggest flop, it sent producer Rutland Barrington into bankruptcy.

The Fortune Hunter (1897). Its reception provoked WSG to announce retiring from writing for the stage.

The Fairy's Dilemma (1904).

The Hooligan (1911).

German Reed Entertainments

Gilbert wrote six one-act musical entertainments for the German Reeds between 1869 and 1875. They were successful in their own right and also helped form Gilbert's mature style as a dramatist.

No Cards (1869)

Ages Ago (1869). Gilbert's first collaboration with Frederic Clay, ran for 350 performances.

Our Island Home (1870)

A Sensation Novel (1871)

Happy Arcadia (1872)

Eyes and No Eyes (1875)

Early Comic Operas

The Gentleman in Black (1870; music by Frederic Clay). The score is lost.

Les Brigands (1871), an English adaptation of Jacques Offenbach's operetta.

Topsyturveydom (1874; music by Alfred Cellier). The score is lost.
Princess Toto (1876; music by Frederic Clay). A three-act opera.

Later Operas (Without Sullivan)
Though not as popular as the works with Arthur Sullivan, a few of Gilbert's later works arguably have stronger plots than the last two Gilbert and Sullivan operas.

The Mountebanks (1892; music; Alfred Cellier). This is the "lozenge plot" that Sullivan declined to set on several occasions.
Haste to the Wedding (1892; music; George Grossmith). An unsuccessful adaptation of The Wedding March.
His Excellency (1894; music; Osmond Carr). Gilbert felt that if Sullivan had set it, the piece would have been "another Mikado".
Fallen Fairies (1909; music by Edward German). Gilbert's last opera, which was a failure.

Parlour Ballads
The Yarn of the Nancy Bell, with music by Alfred Plumpton. One of the Bab Ballads. 1869.
Thady O'Flynn, with music by James L. Molloy. 1868. From No Cards.
Would You Know that Maiden Fair, with music by Frederic Clay. From Ages Ago. c. 1869.
Corisande, with music by James L. Molloy. 1870.
Eily's Reason, with music by James L. Molloy. 1871.
Three songs from A Sensation Novel: "The Detective's Song", "The Tyrannical Bridegroom", and "The Jewel". 1871
The Distant Shore, with music by Arthur Sullivan. 1874.
The Love that Loves me Not, with music by Arthur Sullivan. 1875.
Sweethearts, with music by Arthur Sullivan. 1875.
Let Me Stay, with music by Walter Maynard. 1875.

Arthur Sullivan – His Other Works

Operas
The Sapphire Necklace (ca. 1863; unperformed)
Cox and Box (1866)
The Contrabandista (1867)
The Zoo (1875)
Ivanhoe (1891)
Haddon Hall (1892)
The Chieftain (1894)
The Beauty Stone (1898)
The Rose of Persia (1899)
The Emerald Isle (1901; completed by Edward German)

Incidental Music to Plays

The Tempest (1861)
The Merchant of Venice (1871)
The Merry Wives of Windsor (1874)
Henry VIII (1877)
Macbeth (1888)
Tennyson's The Foresters (1892)
J. Comyns Carr's King Arthur for Henry Irving (1895)

Sheet Music

Ballets and Song Cycle
L'Île Enchantée (1864 ballet)
Victoria and Merrie England (1897 ballet)
The Window; or, The Song of the Wrens (1871 song cycle)

Choral Works with Orchestra
The Masque at Kenilworth (1864)
The Prodigal Son (Sullivan) (1869)
On Shore and Sea (1871)
Festival Te Deum (1872)
The Light of the World (Sullivan) (1873)
The Martyr of Antioch (1880)
Ode for the Opening of the Colonial and Indian Exhibition (1886)
The Golden Legend (1886)
Ode for the Laying of the Foundation Stone of The Imperial Institute (1887)
Te Deum Laudamus (1902; performed posthumously)

Orchestral Works
Overture in D (1858; now lost)
Overture The Feast of Roses (1860; now lost)
Procession March (1863)
Princess of Wales's March (1863)
Symphony in E, "Irish" (1866)
Overture in C, "In Memoriam" (1866)
Concerto for Cello and Orchestra (1866)
Overture Marmion (1867)
Overture di Ballo (1870)
Imperial March (1893)
The Absent-Minded Beggar March (1899)

Other Works

Songs & Parlour Ballads
Absent-minded Beggar (Rudyard Kipling) 1899

Arabian Love Song (Percy Bysshe Shelley) 1866
Ay de mi, My Bird (George Eliot)1874
Bid me at least Goodbye (Sydney Grundy) 1894
Birds in the Night (Lionel H. Lewin) 1869
Bride from the North (Henry F. Chorley) 1863
Care is all Fiddle-dee-dee (F. C. Burnand) 1874
Chorister, The (Fred. E. Weatherly) 1876
Christmas Bells at Sea (C. L. Kenney) 1875
County Guy (Walter Scott) 1867
Distant Shore, The (W. S. Gilbert) 1874
Dove Song (William Brough) 1869
E tu nol sai - see You Sleep (G. Mazzucato) 1889
Edward Gray (Alfred Tennyson)(1880
Ever (Mrs Bloomfield Moore) 1887
First Departure - see The Chorister (Rev. E. Munroe) 1874
Give (Adelaide Anne Procter) 1867
Golden Days (Lionel H. Lewin)1872
Guinevere! (Lionel H. Lewin) 1872
I Heard the Nightingale (Rev. C. H. Townsend) 1863
I Wish to Tune my Quiv'ring Lyre (Anacreon; trans. Lord Byron) 1868
I Would I were a King (Victor Hugo; trans. A. Cockburn) 1878
Ich möchte hinaus es jauchzen (A. Corrodi) 1859
If Doughty Deeds (Robert Graham of Gartmore) 1866
In the Summers Long Ago (J. P. Douglas) 1867
Let Me Dream Again (B. C. Stephenson) 1875
Lied, mit Thränen halbgeschrieben (Eichendorff)1861
Life that Lives for You (Lionel H. Lewin) 1870
Little Darling Sleep Again (Cradle Song) (anon) 1874
Living Poems (H. W. Longfellow)1874
Longing for Home (Jean Ingelow) 1904
Looking Back (Louisa Gray)1870
Looking Forward (Louisa Gray) 1873
Lost Chord, The (Adelaide Anne Procter) 1877
Love that Loves Me Not, The (W. S. Gilbert) 1875
Maiden's Story, The (Emma Embury) 1867
Marquis de Mincepie, The (F. C. Burnand) 1874
Mary Morison (Robert Burns) 1874
Moon in Silent Brightness, The (Bishop Reginald Heber) 1868
Mother's Dream, The (Rev. W. Barnes) 1868
My Dear and Only Love (Marquis of Montrose) 1874
My Dearest Heart (anon) 1874
My Heart is like a Silent Lute (Benjamin Disraeli) 1904
My Love - see "There Sits a Bird in Yonder Tree
My Love Beyond the Sea - see "In the Summers Long Ago"
None but I Can Say (Lionel H. Lewin)1872
O Fair Dove, O Fond Dove (Jean Ingelow) 1868
O Israel (Hosea) 1855
O Mistress Mine (William Shakespeare) 1866

O Swallow, Swallow (Alfred Tennyson) 1900
Oh Sweet and Fair (A. F. C. K.) 1868
Oh! bella mia - see "Oh! Ma Charmante"
Oh! Ma Charmante (Victor Hugo) 1872
Old Love Letters (S. K. Cowen) 1879
Once Again (Lionel H. Lewin) 1872
Orpheus with his Lute (William Shakespeare) 1866
River, The (anon) 1875
Roads Should Blossom, The (anon) 1864
Rosalind (William Shakespeare) 1866
Sad Memories (C. J. Rowe) 1869
Sailor's Grave, The (H. F. Lyte) 1872
St. Agnes' Eve (Alfred Tennyson) 1879
Shadow, A. (Adelaide Anne Procter)1886
She is not Fair to Outward View (Hartley Coleridge) 1866
Sigh no More, Ladies (William Shakespeare) 1866
Sleep My Love, Sleep (R. Whyte Melville) 1874
Snow Lies White, The (Jean Ingelow) 1868
Sometimes (Lady Lindsay of Balcarres) 1877
Sweet Day So Cool (George Herbert) 1864
Sweet Dreamer - see "Oh! Ma Charmante"
Sweethearts (W. S. Gilbert) 1875
Tears, Idle Tears (Alfred Tennyson) 1900
Tender and True (Dinah Maria Mulock) 1874
There Sits a Bird on Yonder TreeRev. (C. H. Barham) 1873
Thou art Lost to Me (anon) 1865
Thou art Weary (Adelaide Anne Procter) 1874
Thou'rt Passing Hence (Felicia Hemans) 1875
To One in Paradise (Edgar Allan Poe) 1904
Troubadour, The (Walter Scott) 1869
Village Chimes, The (C. J. Rowe) 1870
Weary Lot is Thine, Fair Maid, A (Walter Scott) 1866
We've Ploughed our Land (anon)1875
When Thou Art Near (W. J. Stewart) 1877
White Plume, The - see "The Bride from the North"
Will He Come? (Adelaide A. Procter) 1865
Willow Song, The (William Shakespeare)1866
You Sleep (B. C. Stephenson) 1889

Hymns (Title & First Line)
Adoro Te - Saviour, again to Thy dear name we raise (Arranger)
All This Night - All this night bright angels sing
Angel Voices - Angel voices, ever singing
Audite Audientes me - I heard the voice of Jesus say
Bethlehem - While shepherd's watched their flocks (Arranger)
Bishopgarth - O King of Kings, Whose reign of old
Bolwell - Thou to whom the sick and dying

Carrow - My God, I thank Thee Who has made
Chapel Royal - O love that wilt not let me go
Christus - Show me not only Jesus dying
Clarence - Winter reigneth o'er the land
Coena Domini - Draw nigh, and take the body of the Lord
Come Unto Me - Come unto Me, ye weary (Arranger)
Constance - I've found a Friend; oh, such a Friend
Coronae - Crown Him, with many crowns
Courage, Brother - Courage, brother, do not stumble
Dominion Hymn - God bless our wide dominion
Dulce Sonans - Angel voices, ever singing
Ecclesia - The church has waited long
Ellers - Saviour, again to Thy dear name we raise (Arranger)
Evelyn - In the hour of my distress
Ever Faithful - Let us with a gladsome mind
Fatherland (St. Edmund) - I'm but a stranger here
Formosa (Falfield) - Love Divine, all love excelling
Fortunatus - Welcome, happy morning!
Golden Sheaves - To Thee, O Lord, our hearts we raise
Hanford - Jesu, my Saviour, look on me
Heber (Gennesareth) - When through the torn sail
Holy City - Sing Alleluia forth in duteous praise
Hushed was the Evening Hymn - Hushed was the evening hymn
Hymn of the Homeland - The homeland, the homeland
Lacrymae - Lord, in this Thy mercy's day
Leominster - A few more years shall roll (Arranger)
Light - Holy Spirit! Come in might! (Arranger)
Litany (1) - Jesu, life of those who die
Litany (2) - Jesu, we are far away
Long Home, The - Tender Shepherd, Thou hast still'd
Lux eoi - All is bright and cheeful round us
Lux in Tenebris - Lead, kindly Light
Lux Mundi - O Jesu, Thou art standing
Marlborough - O Strength and Stay, upholding all creation (Arranger)
Mount Zion - Rock of Ages, cleft for me
Nearer Home - For ever with the Lord (Arranger)
Noel - It came upon the midnight clear (Arranger)
Old 137th - Great King of nations, hear our prayer (Arranger)
Paradise - O Paradise!
Parting - With the sweet word of peace (Arranger)
Pilgrimage - From Egypt's bondage come
Promissio Patris - Our blest Redeemer, ere He breathed
Propior Deo - Nearer, my God, to Thee
Rest - Art thou weary, art thou languid
Resurrexit - Christ is risen!
Roseate Hues, The - The roseate hues of early dawn
Safe Home - Safe home, safe home in port
St. Ann - The Son of God goes forth to war (Arranger)

St. Francis - O Father, who hast created all
St. Gertrude - Onward, Christian soldiers
St. Kevin - Come, ye faithful, raise the strain
St. Lucian - Of Thy love some gracious token
St. Luke (St. Nathaniel) - God moves in a mysterious way
St. Mary Magdalene - Saviour, when in dust to Thee
St. Millicent - Let no tears to-day be shed
St. Patrick - He is gone - a cloud of light
St. Theresa - Brightly gleams our banner
Saints of God - The Saints of God, their conflict past.
Springtime - For all Thy love and goodness (Arranger)
Strain Upraise, The - The Strain upraise in joy and praise
Thou God of Love - Thou God of Love, beneath Thy sheltering wing
Ultor Omnipotens - God the all terrible! King who ordainest
Valete - Sweet Saviour, bless us 'ere we go
Veni, Creator - Come Holy Ghost, our souls inspire
Victoria - To mourn our dead we gather here

Part Songs

The term "Part Song" is more usually applied to one where the highest part carries the melody with the other voices supplying the accompanying harmonies.

Also included here are the soprano duet, The Sisters, and the trio Sullivan composed for the play Olivia by W. G. Wills, Morn, Happy Morn.

O Lady Dear (Madrigal) - Composed 1857, unpublished.
It was a Lover and his Lass - Words by Shakespeare. Performed at the Royal Academy of Music, 1857, unpublished.
Seaside Thoughts - Words by Bernard Bartram. Composed 1857. Published 1904.
The Last Night of the Year - Words by H. F. Chorley. Published 1863.
O Hush Thee, My Babie - Words by Walter Scott. Published 1867.
The Rainy Day - Words by H. W. Longfellow. Published 1867.
Evening - Words by Lord Houghton, after Goethe. Published 1868.
Parting Gleams - Words by Aubrey de Vere. Published 1868.
Echoes - Words by Thomas Moore. Published 1868.
The Long Day Closes - Words by H. F. Chorley. Published 1868.
Joy to the Victors - Words by Walter Scott. Published 1868
The Beleaguered - Words by H. F. Chorley. Published 1868.
It Came Upon the Midnight Clear - Words by E. H. Sears. Published 1871.
Lead, Kindly Light - Words by J. H. Newman. Published 1871.
Through Sorrows Path - Words by H. Kirke White. Published 1871.
Say, Watchman, What of the Night? - Words from Isaiah. Published 1871.
The Way is Long and Dreary - Words by Adelaide Anne Procter. Published 1871.
Morn, Happy Morn - Composed for the play, Olivia by W. G. Wills. Published 1878.
The Sisters - Words by Alfred Tennyson. Published 1881.
Wreaths for our Graves - Words by L. F. Massey. Published 1898.

Fair Daffodils - Words by Robert Herrick. Published 1904.

Church Songs
By the Waters of Babylon - Composed c. 1850. Unpublished.
Sing unto the Lord - Composed 1855. Unpublished.
Psalm 103 - Composed 1856. Unpublished.
We have heard with our ears
(i) Dedicated to Sir George Smart and performed at the Chapel Royal, January 1860.
(ii) Dedicated to Rev. Thomas Helmore. 1865.
O Love the Lord - Dedicated to John Goss. 1864.
Te Deum, Jubilate, Kyrie (in D major) 1866.
O God, Thou art Worthy - Composed for the wedding of Adrian Hope, 3 June 1867. Published in 1871.
O Taste and See - Dedicated to Rev. C. H. Haweis. 1867.
Rejoice in the Lord - Composed for the wedding of Rev. R. Brown-Borthwick, 16 April 1868.
Sing, O Heavens - Dedicated to Rev. F. C. Byng. 1869.
I Will Worship - Dedicated to Rev. F. Gore Ouseley. 1871.
Two Choruses adapted from Russian Church Music, 1874.
(i) Turn Thee Again
(ii) Mercy and Truth
I Will Mention Thy Loving-kindness - Dedicated to John Stainer. 1875.
I Will Sing of Thy Power. 1877.
Hearken Unto Me, My People. 1877.
Turn Thy Face. 1878.
Who is Like unto Thee - Dedicated to Walter Parratt. 1883.
I Will Lay Me Down in Peace - Composed 1868. Published only in 1910.

Christmas Carols & Songs

Advent
Hearken unto me, my people - An Anthem for Advent or General Use. Words from Isaiah. (1877)

Christmas Carols
All this night bright angels sing - Words by W. Austin. (1870)
I Sing the Birth - Words by Ben Jonson. (1868)
It Came Upon the Midnight Clear - Words by E. H. Sears.
Part Song for Soprano Solo and Choir (1871)
Hymn Tune "Noel" (1874)
Upon the Snow-clad Earth (1876)
While Shepherds Watched - Words by Nahum Tate (1874)
Hark! What Mean those Holy Voices? - Words by John Cawood (1883)

Songs
Christmas Bells at Sea - Words by Charles Kenney (1875)

Two songs from The Miller and His Man - A Christmas Drawing Room Entertainment. Words by F. C. Burnand (1874)
The Marquis de Mincepie
Care is all Fiddle-dee-dee
The Last Night of the Year - Part Song - Words by H. F. Chorley (1863)

Chamber Music & Solo Piano
Scherzo - Piano Solo, 1857, unpublished.
Capriccio No. 2 - Piano Solo (unfinished), 1857, unpublished.
String Quartet - Performed at Leipzig, May 1859. Published 2000
Romance in G minor - For string quartet, 1859. Published 1964.
Thoughts - Two pieces for piano solo, Published by Cramer, 1862.
An Idyll - For Cello and Piano. Composed in 1865 and Published 1899.
Allegro Risoluto - Piano solo, 1866. Published only in 1974
Berceuse - Based on the theme of Hushed was the Bacon from Cox and Box but with additional material.
Day Dreams - Six pieces for piano solo. 1867
Duo Concertante - Cello and piano. 1868
Twilight - Piano solo. 1868

www.ingramcontent.com/pod-product-compliance
Lightning Source LLC
Chambersburg PA
CBHW060144050426
42448CB00010B/2292